THE LOST CHRONICLE OF BARNSTAPLE

1586–1611

An extract of some particulars of
towne clarke's of mr Adam Wyatt's booke (beinge a journall
of things observeable in and about Barstaple,
from An. Dom. 1586. unto An. 1611.

1586. By the infection of the prisoners that were
arraigned the assises at Exeter before Easter,
last, which were sick of the gaoll sicknes,
many men of worship and other that were
ther at that time shortly after dyed therof
viz. one of the Justices of the assises called
mr Baron Flowerdewe, sir Arthur
Basset knight sir John Chichester and sir
Barnard Drake knights and mr Walrond, mr
Cary of Clavelly, mr Cary of Hackome, mr
Fortiscue, mr Thomas Risdon Justices of
peace and diverse others of this Shire of
Devon. &c.

On Michaelmas eve this year the weather being
very fowle, ther arose such a tempest of
winde, that it made the water at the kay
so arise, that they that were upon the kay
and saw it, could not see the marsh: it
went upward and ripped diverse houses between mr Wourthy lane and the fish shambles.

Frontispiece. The first page of Adam Wyatt's chronicle copied by Jonathan Hanmer, mid 17th century.

THE LOST CHRONICLE OF BARNSTAPLE 1586–1611

EDITED
WITH AN INTRODUCTION BY

TODD GRAY
BA, PhD, FRHistS

1998

British Library Cataloguing in Publication Data
A catalogue entry of this book is available from the British Library.

ISBN 0 85214 063 0

Designed and typeset for the Association by
Colin Bakké Typesetting, Exeter
and printed and bound for the Association by
Short Run Press Ltd, Exeter
United Kingdom

FOR THE
PEOPLE OF BARNSTAPLE

CONTENTS

LIST OF MAPS AND ILLUSTRATIONS

Maps

Illustrations

ACKNOWLEDGEMENTS

I am greatly indebted to the staff in the Somerset Record Office, in particular Tom Mayberry, Robin Harcourt Williams and the staff of the North Devon Record Office, North Devon Athenaeum and Devon Record Office for their help in providing documents. I would like to thank Dr Jonathan Barry, Dr Alison Grant, Dr Tom Greeves, Dr Alexandra Walsham, Tim Wormleighton and Professor Joyce Youings for their assistance and comments on the Introduction and Professor Patrick Collinson for his support. I am also grateful to Eileen Cox and Jacqueline Brooks who typed Palmer's copy of the Chronicle and thereby saved me many hours of work. I am grateful to Professor Youings for supplying illustration 18, James Coulter for 10, 13, 17, 25 & 26, and Alison Mills for 11 & 24. For permission to publish the texts and illustrations I would like to thank the Marquess of Salisbury, Somerset Record Office, North Devon Record Office, Museum of North Devon, University of Exeter and the Trustees of the North Devon Athenaeum. I would also like to thank Andrew Taggart of Park Community School, Barnstaple, who coordinated the drawing competition and whose students' work is in this book, and of course the students themselves. Many other individuals gave their time and among them I would like to particularly thank Norman Annett and James Coulter and the members of the North Devon Branch of the Devonshire Association. Finally, I would like to thank the trustees of Barnstaple Bridge Trust and Barnstaple Town Council, in particular Bill Forward and Mike Taylor, for their financial help and general support which has made this book possible.

FOREWORD

BY EMERITUS PROFESSOR JOYCE YOUINGS
PHD, HON. DLITT., FRHISTS

Historians have long dreamed of finding the original manuscript of the journal kept by the late-Elizabethan and early-Stuart Town Clerk of Barnstaple, the text of which has been known until now only from an incomplete and somewhat unreliable eighteenth-century copy printed well over a century ago and available only to those who knew where to find it. It is unlikely that the original ever will be found, but we now have, in an attractive printed version accessible to all, the next best thing. It took, not the Internet, but the eagle eyes of Dr Todd Gray, to recognize, not a hundred miles from Barnstaple, in the Somerset Record Office at Taunton, a much earlier and considerably fuller copy of the text. Moreover, and it now seems so obvious, the author turns out to be one Adam Wyatt (or Wyott: even he was not sure how to spell it) not Philip, as we have always supposed, who was in fact his father.

Mayors came and went and even Aldermen had their personal affairs to attend to, but as the town's business manager from 1586 right down to 1608, Adam Wyatt possessed a unique knowledge of what was going on and saw it as one of his duties to write, as well as the town's more formal records, a diary of the memorable happenings he had witnessed. These included the arrival of important visitors, shipping movements, floods, outbreaks of the dreaded plague, and, of vital concern to his fellow townsmen, the weather, market prices and the state of the harvest, with only the occasional bit of news from further afield.

He was, indeed, a man for all ages and his chronicle a window on Barnstaple's world.

Todd Gray has not only provided a text of Wyatt's chronicle which is as near the original as we are ever likely to achieve but for the first time, while retaining the original grammar and spelling which gives it its flavour, has provided authoritative explanatory notes which makes it readable and enjoyable even by those who would claim to know little about life in a small provincial town four hundred years ago. The editor, the Devonshire Association and all who have made this publication possible, are to be warmly congratulated.

INTRODUCTION

THE CHRONICLE is Barnstaple's single most important document in that it reveals much of the town's history, and that of the surrounding hinterland, over the course of twenty-five years during what may be called its 'Golden Age'. More than one hundred years ago one historian recognized the Chronicle as:

> a most valuable document to all subsequent historians of Barnstaple, but has much general interest as a curious delineation of habits of life and manners of that early period.[1]

But it has importance far beyond Barnstaple or north Devon: those who are interested in urban, social and maritime history will gain much from examining the account of events as viewed by the town clerk. Its significance lies partly in that it provides noteworthy information not found elsewhere, for example the reference to five ships sailing to fight against the Armada has been enthusiastically quoted by generations of historians.[2] Many other references are unexpected such as a note of the reopening of the Combe Martin silver mine which had been inactive for generations until the discovery of a rich lode and the subsequent investment of Sir Adrian Gilbert. Nearly all provide vivid images such as in 1596 when it was noted that:

> In the beginning of this month May divers salt petre makers [arrived] with commission to enter into houses & places to dig & delve upp the earth to make the peter, and do make salt peter thereof and clear salt, they take the earth dug up and cast water thereunto & so standeth a

> certain tyme. Then they let the water out of the tubb and by a certain tyme after boyl the same in a great furnace. A long tyme then they take it out and put in small vessels to cowle [cool], and thereof cometh the salt peter & salt.

The Chronicle is particularly interesting because of the period which is covered. For seventeen of the twenty-five years the chief overseas markets of the town were closed, war disrupted food supplies and the middle of the 1590s saw unprecedented harvest failure. Against this background of real and potential social unrest there were also great opportunities in the shape of staggering wealth which suddenly materi-

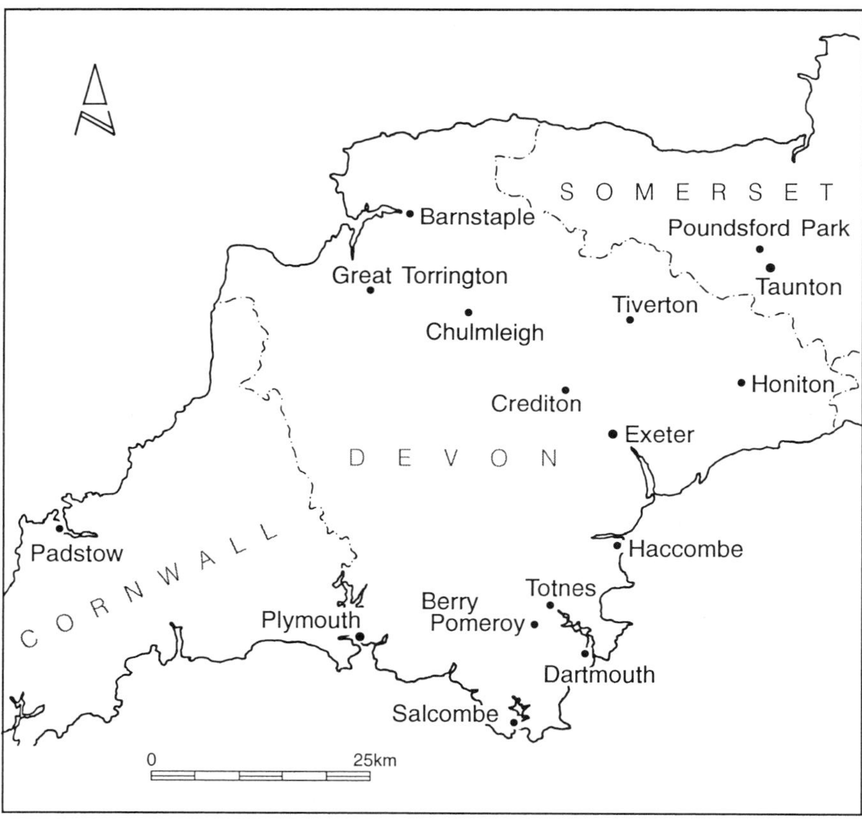

Map 1. Devon.

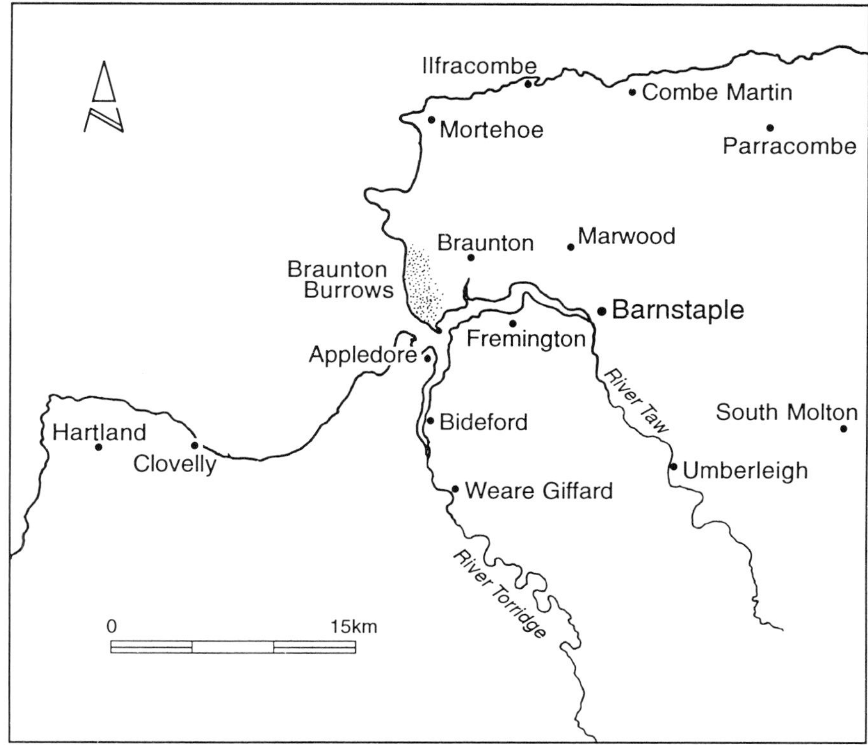

Map 2. North Devon.

alized from privateering voyages. The chronicler observed events which resulted in unexpected and considerable social and economic fluctuations against a background of great changes in the government of the town.

It is not surprising that for two centuries the Chronicle has been cherished and its importance acknowledged, one local historian enthusiastically pronounced Wyatt the 'Pepys of North Devon',[3] and his work has been widely regarded as the central text on Elizabethan Barnstaple. In consequence, generations of historians have relied upon it and paid homage to Philip Wyatt as author. Yet for nearly two hundred years a singular and awkward mistake, albeit understandable, has gone unnoticed and been repeated by generations of historians: the account was not actually written by Philip Wyatt.

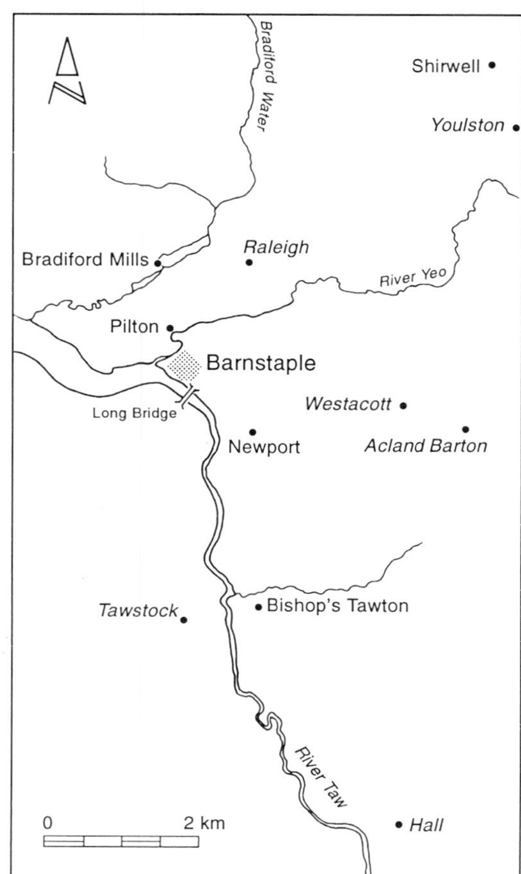

Map 3. Barnstaple and its immediate area.

This misunderstanding has arisen chiefly because of the loss of the original manuscript which may have occurred as early as the late eighteenth century. Its whereabouts remain a mystery although it has been sought for many years.[4] Professor W.G. Hoskins was one of many historians who recognized its importance and implored others to search for the original document.[5] Historians have had to rely upon an edition printed from a copy made in the eighteenth century, possibly in the 1770s. This small quarto book of 52 leaves, measuring 8 inches by 6½ inches, with a parchment cover on which is written 'Extracts', is now held by the North Devon Athenaeum under the care of the North Devon Record Office. It claims to be 'extracts from an old manuscript in the possession of William Palmer of Barnstaple, clerk, wrote by Philip Wyot, town clerk of Barnstaple, beginning at the years 1586 to 1608'. Palmer was mayor in 1613, 1631 and in 1642.[6] Presumably it was still in the care of a town official when copied and subsequently lost. One possible clue to its whereabouts was suggested in 1942: William Matthews then claimed in his *British Diaries, 1442–1942*[7] that it was in the possession of one Mr Alfred James but his heirs did not find the manuscript among his papers.[8]

In 1866 John Roberts Chanter printed the text of Palmer's copy. He thought it was compiled from Philip Wyatt's annual pocket books. Chanter also noted that the copy subsequently belonged to Mounieur Roch, 'a scholar and antiquarian, son of one of the French refugees who settled here', before being given to Chanter's grandfather some sixty years before. On the inside cover of the manuscript is a note by John Roberts, Chanter's grandfather, that Mounieur Roch died 7 January 1807 and his widow on 27 September 1810. A further note claims that the manuscript was given by Mrs Yeo, a 'representative' of Mrs Roch.[9] The manuscript was inherited by Chanter's son, J.F. Chanter, the rector of Parracombe and canon and prebendary of Exeter Cathedral, and given by him to the North Devon Athenaeum in about 1926.[10]

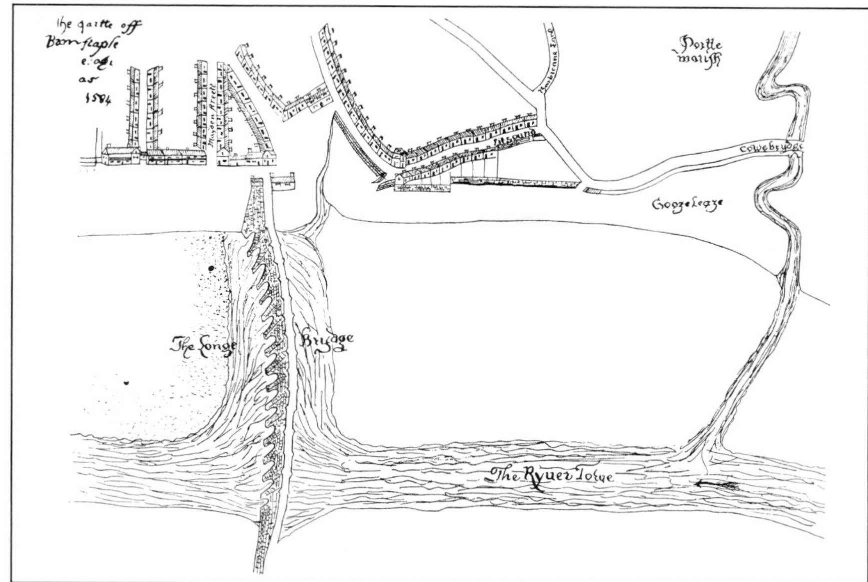

Map 4. River front of Barnstaple in 1584 as depicted in a map whose origins are uncertain. Only a copy remains in the North Devon Athenaeum.

This copy has always been recognized as incomplete. Some entries are numbered and the gaps indicate there were originally some 170 entries leaving the possibility that portions of the original were not copied. Recently another copy, hereafter called the Hanmer copy after its author, has come to light.[11] The style of handwriting indicates it was written in the middle of the seventeenth century. It is not nearly as lengthy as Palmer's copy but it nevertheless helps us to understand the original Chronicle and the additional passages provide further details on Barnstaple.

The Identity of the Compiler

The most immediate information Hanmer's copy imparts is that the Chronicle was the work of Adam Wyatt, a close relation of Philip's. There are many corroborative references within the text which establishes that it was written by Adam and not Philip Wyatt, notably referring to family connections, but Hanmer's copy actually begins with the

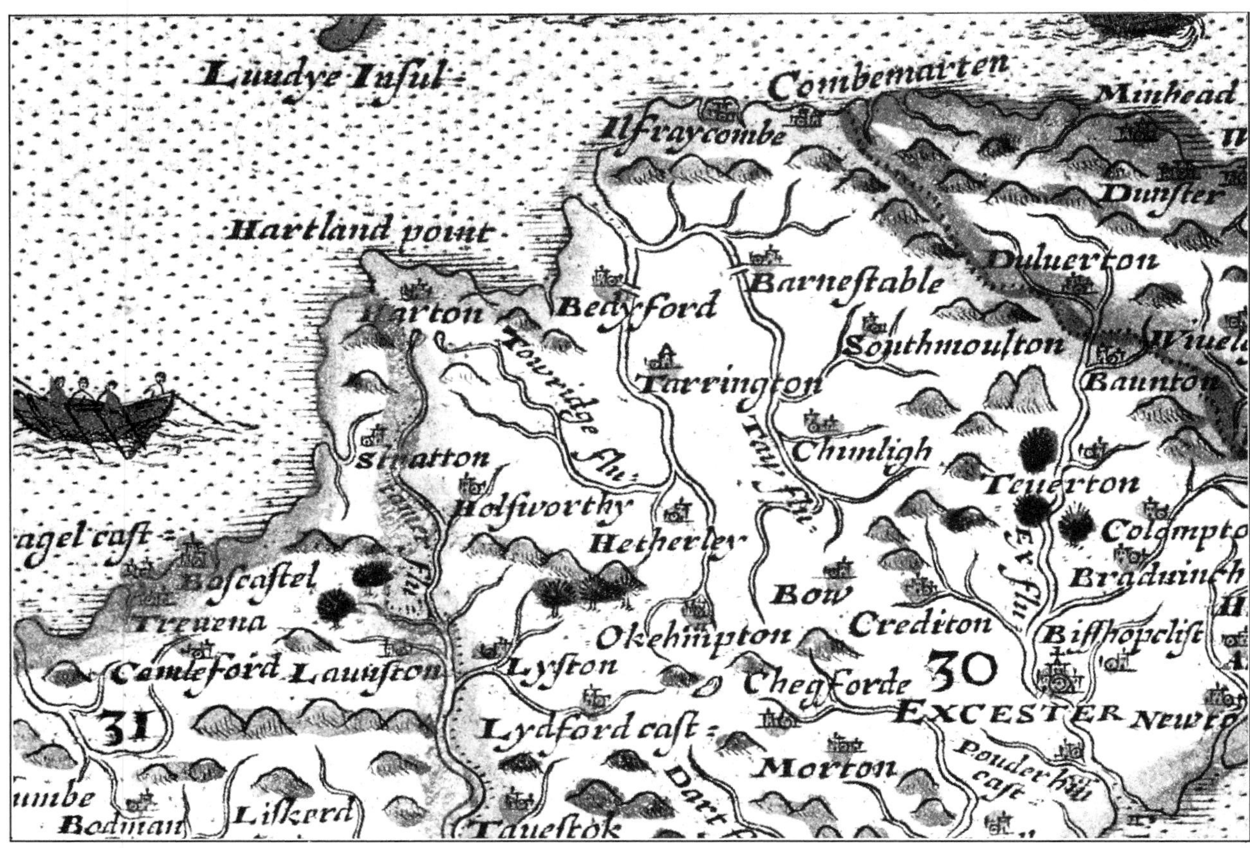

Map 5. Detail of Christopher Saxton's map of Devon, 1579 (University of Exeter).

assertion that Adam Wyatt was the original compiler. The name Adam was substituted for that of Philip in the heading.

The original mistake lay with the eighteenth-century copyist who attributed the work to Philip Wyatt and this was repeated in print in the first part of the nineteenth century. In 1822 Daniel and Samuel Lysons merely noted that it was 'kept by a town clerk of Barnstaple'[12] but in 1824 the *North Devon Magazine* credited Philip Wyatt with authorship. There were understandable grounds for confusion: Barnstaple appointed one Philip Wyatt as town clerk in 1558 and another as deputy recorder in 1653. Adam Wyatt directly succeeded Philip Wyatt upon his father's death in 1586. The Wyatt family kept the office of town clerk for 53 continuous years and they were not unique in maintaining such a hold: for instance their counterparts in Stratford-upon-Avon were the Hunt family.[13]

But more to the point, Philip was a common Christian name in the Wyatt family and was the name of Adam's father, brother and nephew.[14] Only some of the confusion can be placed on the original's loss given that the text clearly shows that it was not possible for Philip (the father) to have compiled it as he died too early, or Philip (the nephew) because he was born the year that the account began.[15] Of the three Philips, only Adam's brother could have written the Chronicle. Hanmer's copy also provides corroborating evidence for the compiler being Adam Wyatt. Palmer's copy covers the years from 1586 to 1608 while the last entry in Hanmer's copy was taken from the year 1609 and two further entries, one of which is for 5 February 1611, are included which were written on a loose sheet of paper found in Wyatt's original manuscript. On the first page of Hanmer's copy is a note that Wyatt maintained his account until 1611. This was the year in which

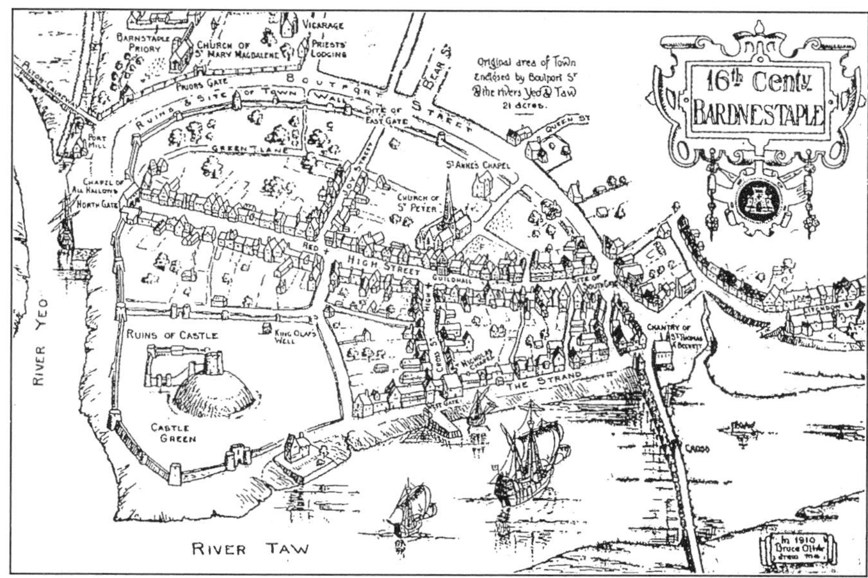

Map 6. Sixteenth-century Barnstaple (Bruce Oliver, 1910).

Adam died; the burial register for Barnstaple recording that he was buried on 10 October 1611. Clearly, Wyatt continued to write until shortly before his death.

It is surprising that neither Chanter nor Thomas Wainwright, first librarian of the North Devon Athenaeum, discovered the author's true identity since both men, particularly Chanter, were familiar with the records of Barnstaple, and the borough receiver's accounts annually specified that Adam Wyatt was town clerk. It was Chanter who investigated the Chronicle more thoroughly than any other historian and subsequent historians have followed their lead, including Sydney Harper who also researched the town clerks and was particularly interested in the Chronicle.[16] Most recently one historian acknowledged that the Herald's Visitation of 1620 introduces 'certain confusion' by noting Adam Wyatt as town clerk but still insisted that Philip Wyatt was the clerk and author in question.[17]

The Definition of a Chronicle

It is not possible to be definitive about the Chronicle's contents because we are still working with an incomplete text and all discussion and analysis of it must keep this in mind. Nevertheless, it is clear that Wyatt was not interested in writing a history of Barnstaple at least not in the sense that John Hooker was of Exeter. It is also markedly different from the county histories which were then being written across the country as well as in Devon by Hooker and shortly afterwards by at least three others.[18] Wyatt's work has generally been referred to as a 'diary' and occasionally as a 'journal', by Chanter among many others, but Hanmer's copy noted it as a 'book (being a journal) of things observable in and about Barnstaple' and ends by referring to it as 'his memorials of the said town'. One writer has even called it 'The Barum Diary'.[19] The diary/book/journal/memorials may most properly be termed a 'Chronicle', a term which Chanter used once,[20] in much the same way as there were others written for several urban areas of Devon (for example, Exeter, Tiverton and Plymouth)[21] as well as for Bristol and many other English towns and cities. As late as the end of

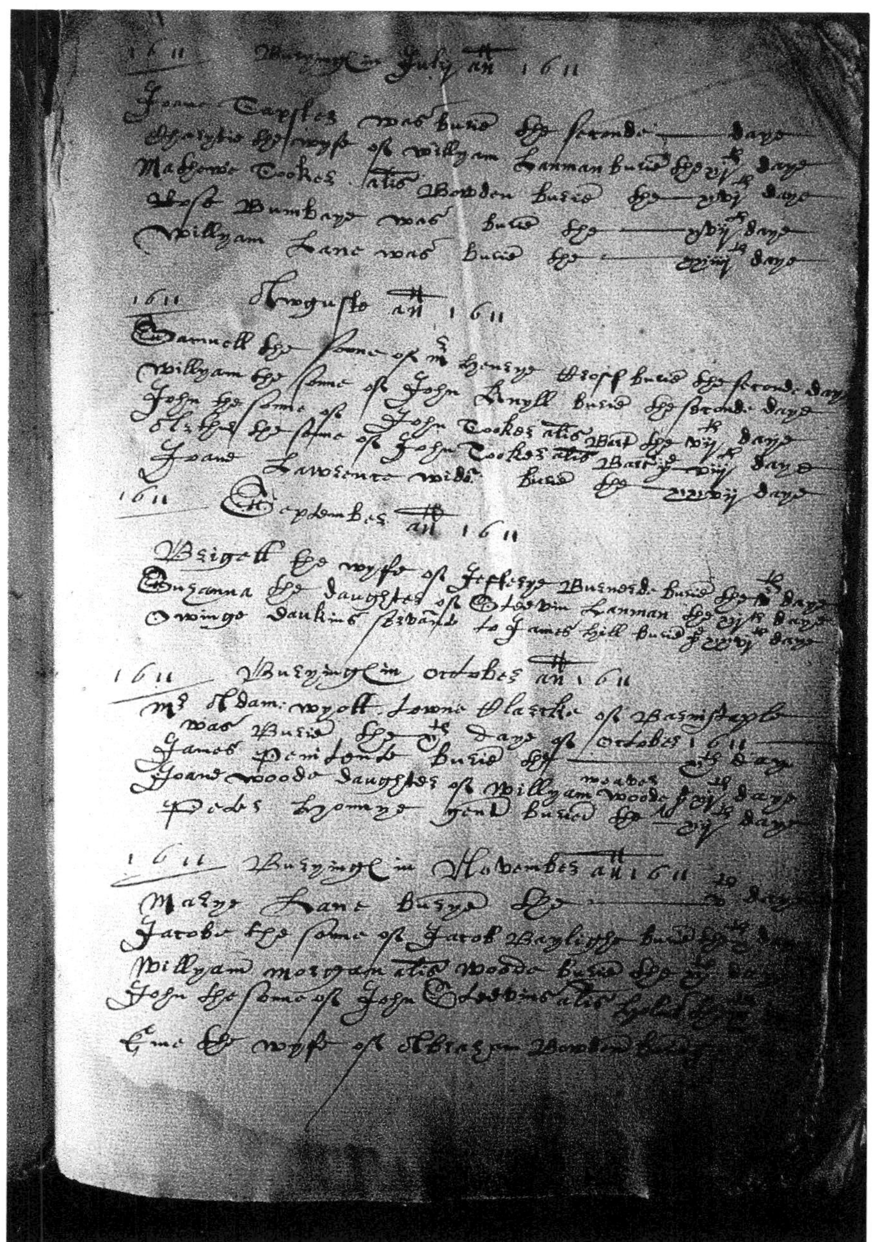

Figure 1. Note of the burial of Adam Wyatt in Barnstaple parish register, 10 October 1611.

the nineteenth century they were still being written locally: in 1880 one was completed for Torquay and Torbay.[22] Chronicles have been defined as 'a chronological listing of the chief officers of the municipality in each year, with the addition of notes of events which occurred during this year of office'.[23] Given that some of the original manuscript was not copied it is difficult to be definitive in categorizing Wyatt's work. It could equally be called an Annal[24] in addition to being defined as either a diary, journal or memorial. But these terms themselves cannot be so strictly classified and the term Chronicle fits better to that part of the work which has survived than any other definition.

A comparison between Wyatt's work with that which was subsequently written by Richard Wood, a vicar of nearby Fremington, shows that Wood read the Chronicle, or a copy of it, made notes and then continued it in an abbreviated fashion. His account, which is reproduced as Appendix II, appears to have been written for purely personal reasons and was itself extended to 1678 by a Mr Frayne, one of the town's receivers.[25]

Wyatt did not compose his work with a compelling awareness of the past; he began writing when appointed as a town official and little in it refers to events or people before then. This is perhaps understandable given the murky nature of Barnstaple's claim to ancient borough status: it has been shown that in the fifteenth century the townsmen misled the government by copying charters given to Exeter and submitting the forgeries as authentic documents.[26] Wyatt may not have had many original manuscripts with which to research Barnstaple's history.

In the late sixteenth century John Hooker, chamberlain for the city of Exeter, wrote a chronology for the years 1216 to 1590. He explained that:

> in the end of every particular Mayor's year there is subnected [subjoined] and written a brief abstract of some such things as were done in that year and especially in these west parts.[27]

After his death Hooker's work was brought up to date by Samuel Izacke[28] and some years later another historian composed a similar work for Tiverton.[29] Hooker had considerable experience: in the 1570s and 1580s he partly wrote *Holinshed's Chronicle*. Dr James Yonge, mayor of Plymouth in the late seventeenth century, also composed for that port a chronology which he began for the fifteenth century.[30]

Wyatt would have been fully aware that even as he recorded life in Barnstaple there were others, many town clerks like himself or his equivalent, who were equally hard at work noting similar events in other towns and cities. In other urban areas of England the compilers were former mayors, bailiffs and, in one instance, coroner.[31] Wyatt made occasional trips to Exeter, only a day's journey from Barnstaple, and would have been aware of John Hooker by reputation if they were not personally acquainted. Such works were written with civic pride and a sense of identity and purpose.

Chronicles were written as a commentary of events within a year-to-year structure and may have become less fashionable in the late sixteenth century as a genre in the writing of history: one writer in 1592 urged his readers to avoid 'lay chronigraphers that write of nothing but of mayors and sheriffs and the dear year and the great frost'.[32] Chronicles preserved information for subsequent civic use and that of Barnstaple was also not written merely for one person's own needs. In one instance Wyatt plainly wrote with the reader in mind: upon being denied the main source of his income by a newly-elected mayor Wyatt stated his case and concluded 'now let every man judge'. In effect Wyatt wrote a civic commonplace book,[33] a record of those particular events in Barnstaple which Wyatt regarded as important enough for future town officials to remember. This purpose is important in attempting to distinguish it from the many personal diaries being written across the country at the time including local ones by Sir Walter Yonge of Colyton or William Whiteway of Dorchester.[34] Wyatt wrote of local events and, unlike his fellow contemporary chroniclers or diarists, very rarely noted national or international ones. Neither is there any evidence that he plagiarized from them. Wyatt's attention was firmly focused upon Barnstaple and its hinterland and when he strayed from it, such as when he noted developments in Irish affairs, the stirring news of Grenville and the *Revenge* or the bringing of a prize ship to Salcombe, the subject directly related to Barnstaple. If he noted the death of Elizabeth or the coronation of James I, for example, the later copyists failed to record it. It is also important to appreciate that Wyatt was not preparing a work for publication, unlike many others then being produced. His account was a functional work and it is important to remember that it began with Wyatt's appointment as town clerk. Perhaps part of the long confusion over the identity of the compiler arose because Adam Wyatt's predecessor also wrote a Chronicle although there is no evidence of it.

Barnstaple's Chronicle was a historical record compiled for civic use, written either as part of Wyatt's duties, from his interest in organizing the town's records or possibly partly as a personal enthusiasm.[35] Some of Wyatt's personality comes through in his writing: he dismissed the result of one dispute in 1599 as 'the most part of this metal in the refining went off in smoke' and certain expenditure he noted as 'a great charge to small effect'. Apparently it was not then intended for the general public although the existence of several later copies establishes that it achieved some popularity and renown not that long after Wyatt's death. As with other chronicles such as those at Bristol, it was probably loaned out to and copied by interested parties.[36]

The History of the Earliest Surviving Copy of the Chronicle

The new copy has seven sheets of paper and measures 3¾ inches by 5½ inches. It can be dated by a note written at the top of the first page, in a later hand, that it was copied by Jonathan Hanmer 'an ejected minister of Bishop's Tawton, Devon in the reign of Charles II'. Hanmer was the rector at nearby Instow in 1632 and afterwards went to Bishop's Tawton. He was subsequently lecturer at Barnstaple, ejected in 1662 and died there on 18 December 1687.[37] Presumably it was during his employment in Barnstaple that he had access to the original Chronicle.

After that date the new copy's ownership can be traced from Hanmer in Barnstaple to its relatively recent deposit at the Somerset Record Office. A note is inscribed on the title page that it was found at Poundsford Park which suggests that the manuscript passed to

Hanmer's grand-daughter Jane who, in 1737, married Isaac Welman of Poundsford Park near Taunton in Somerset and presumably brought the Chronicle with her to her new home. It is at this point that the descent of ownership becomes uncertain. Possibly it was inherited by a member of the Welman family, given as a gift or even merely borrowed but its location remains unknown for two hundred years, until 1936, when it was deposited at the Somerset Record Office by the Sanford family of Chipley Park near Minehead.[38]

Wyatt's Chronicle in Print

Devon's first two topographical historians, who followed on from John Hooker, do not seem to have read Barnstaple's Chronicle but this is understandable given the two men, Tristram Risdon and Thomas Westcote, were near contemporaries of Adam Wyatt.[39] More curious, it does not seem to have been used by the Reverend Richard Polwhele in his *History of Devonshire*[40] in 1793 but first appeared by the Lysons brothers in their *Magna Britannia* in 1822,[41] then in the *North Devon Magazine containing The Cave and Lundy Review*[42] in 1824 and by Joseph Besly Gribble in his *Memorials of Barnstaple* in 1830.[43] These were all portions of the copy. Finally in 1866 J.R. Chanter published Palmer's copy of the Chronicle in its entirety in his *Sketches of Some Striking Incidents in the History of Barnstaple*.[44]

As early as 1810, when the Lysons brothers were in north Devon, the original manuscript's location was uncertain; they wrote 'there are two or three copies in Barnstaple, although the original appears to have been mislaid'.[45] The unnamed contributor to the *North Devon Magazine* printed abstracts up to the year 1595 and may have intended to publish the rest at a later date. It is possible that he had an additional version because there are some superficial differences in the texts but closer inspection suggests that these resulted from his editing the original account: while his transcript provides further dates it appears these were mainly the result of some confusion over sequential numbering in the original.

Both Hanmer and Palmer summarized extracts from the original. Whereas Palmer's copy noted in 1588:

> 110 fat oxen in the market one day, the like never seen before on Friday before Easter.

in Hanmer's copy it was recorded:

> *An*[*no*] 1588 upon the Friday before Passion Sunday there were here in the market about 110 fat bėeves and above, the like number had not been seen before in the market the like day.

Likewise, there is a similar difference in the report of the last battle of Sir Richard Grenville aboard the *Revenge*. In Palmer's copy it was noted that:

> same day report came that her Majesty's ship at sea Sir Richard Greynfild Captain was taken by the Spaniards after encountering the whole Spanish Fleet for 2 days.

while Hanmer's copy recorded that:

> *An*[*no*] 1591. Sir Rich: Greynfield in the *Revenge* one of the queens ships about the beginning of Sept. encountered with the whole Spanish fleet being 70 sail whereof they slew many men but were fain to yield at last upon composition for their lives and liberties. This fight began in the afternoon, continued all the next night and until ten of the clock the next day.

Likewise Palmer's copy refers to a flood in 1586 merely as being 'very high' in September and that the wind was from the west. Hanmer's copy recorded:

> On Michaelmas eve this year the weather being very fowl, there arose such a tempest of wind, that it made the water at the quay so arise, that they that were upon the quay and saw it could not see the marsh: it went upward and ripped diverse houses between Mr Worth's lane and the

Figure 2. 'Cattle in the market' by Miranda Hill, Year 8, Park Community School, Barnstaple, 1998.

fish-shambles and so in that breadth in it went east through the town blowing down much covering of houses: it was about 4 of the clock in the afternoon.

Hanmer's copy also provides new subjects. One such entry refers to an earthquake early in the morning of Tuesday, the 19th of May, in 1607 when the earth and houses 'did quiver and shake, for a small time,

Figure 3. Cover illustration of the pamphlet of the flood along the Bristol Channel, 1607.

yet no hurt done'. Another 'new' piece of information is Wyatt's note of the mayor taking financial liberties and there is also a reference to an unfortunate birth of twins, one of whom died.

There is also evidence which indicates that both versions paraphrased the original: there are considerable differences in the descriptions of the great flood of 1607 and each provides slightly differing and unique details.

In 1824 the Chronicle was turned into verse as 'The Spirit of the North Devon Journals' in the *North Devon Magazine containing the Cave and Lundy Review* and has been reproduced here as Appendix I. It began:

> Come all you Barum constables, come lawyers clerk and gowned clerk!
> I've got a little song to sing about a gentle Town-clerk;
> And if the name of Philip Wyat mingle in my story,
> Tis all with due submission to that old quill-barber's glory.

According to the writer, the spirit of the town clerk appeared to him and related the history of the town. He penned:

> Just where the evening shadows fell within a book-recess
> Upstarted Philip Wyatt, in his old and clerkly dress;
> Black was his coat, around his throat there was a ruff and band,
> A goose-quill stuck behind his ear—a Journal in his hand.
>
> Three strides he made into the room in front of my tea-table
> And I rose up to set a chair—as well as I was able;
> Of this he took no notice, but in a tone commanding,
> Said 'take your pen and follow me!' then read his journal standing.

The Town of Barnstaple

By 1600 Barnstaple had no more than 2,000 residents, and probably considerably less. It was smaller than Exeter or Plymouth but similar in size to other Devon market towns such as Dartmouth or Crediton.[46] In the first part of the sixteenth century it was perceived to have become rather decayed but by the end of the century John Hooker thought it not only the 'chief emporium' of north Devon but '[ac]counted a little city for it hath all things in it as in a city'.[47]

In the 1630s Barnstaple was described as:

> pleasantly and sweetly situate amidst hills, in form of a semi-circle, upon the river, as it were a diameter, whose streets, in whatsoever weather, are clean and fairly paved.[48]

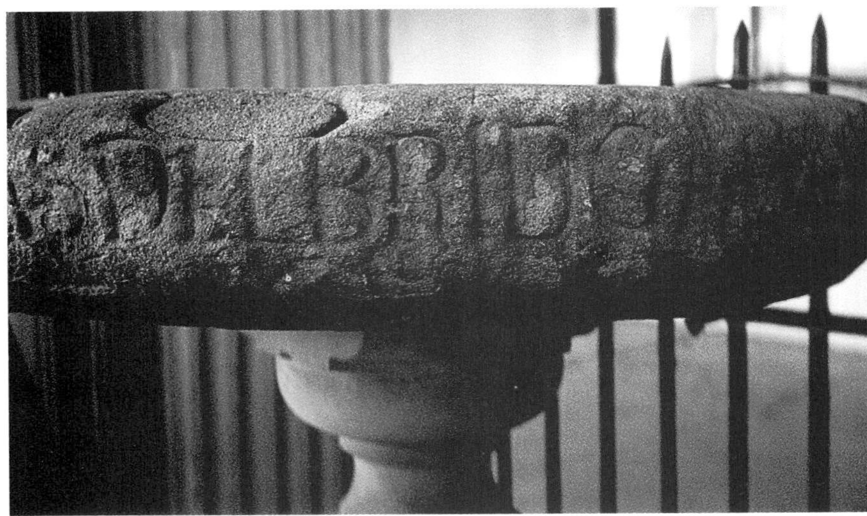

Figure 4. The tomb stone, where merchants agreed upon business deals, with the name 'John Delbridge' cut into the stone, early seventeenth century. Now in Queen Anne's Walk.

It has been called the 'Town of Bridges' for to its west lies the river Taw, to the south the Coney stream and to the north the river Yeo. In the early seventeenth century the latter was remembered in verse:

> To a town for situation delightsome to the eye,
> Thro' pleasant meads and marshes Taw merrily doth hye,
> Which furnished with traffick is, and merchandise so good,
> For that her stream is intermix'd with Severn's swelling flood,
> Yet Barnstaple grac'd, tho' thou be by the brackish Taw,
> In all thy glory see thou not forget the little *Yeaw*.[49]

The only approach from land is to the east. Long Bridge[50] crosses the greater of the rivers, the Taw, and the town's position on its north bank is only five miles from where the Taw meets the river Torridge and a short distance from the great sands of Braunton Burrows and from the Bristol Channel. The sandbar at the mouth of the two rivers has presented navigational difficulties for many generations; there are many entries of drownings in the burial registers for the surrounding parishes, one example is that for the burials of three men, from a vessel 'of the Forest', in 1578.[51] During his boyhood in Braunton, at the mouth of the rivers Taw and Torridge, Wyatt would have walked to the Burrows to watch Barnstaple's ships cross the bar and sail out of sight. Barnstaple's greatest drawback with the river was the continual threat of flooding, Wyatt recorded two such disasters to life and property.

Barnstaple was compact, centred around the Guildhall and the parish church of St Peter and St Mary Magdalene, extending along the river from the Castle to Long Bridge. The Strand, then a long beach, was developed in the late sixteenth century in order to berth ships for the continental and transatlantic voyages. Wyatt noted, and mostly approved of, the continual changes.

While Exeter has always had the preeminent position as the county's religious and judicial centre, Barnstaple had some status as an archdeaconry and the county assizes occasionally came to the town. Then, as now, it was the main market for north Devon and the area's commercial centre. There was great diversity between the Devon ports: the character of Barnstaple was different from Plymouth which traded

Figure 5. 'The *White Hart* at Ilfracombe' by Christopher David, Year 7, Park Community School, Barnstaple, 1998.

chiefly with Portuguese and Spanish ports and was increasingly influenced in its development by its strategic naval role, Dartmouth which was dominated by overseas fishing, and Exeter which was chiefly interested in trade with the northern French ports and had the greatest share of cloth exports. Barnstaple had a greater mix in its commercial activities. In the years before Adam Wyatt moved from Braunton to

Figure 6. 'The hanging of candles and lanterns' by Steven Ashford, Year 8, Park Community School, Barnstaple, 1998.

Barnstaple the town had become wealthy through trade in cloth and north Atlantic fish to ports in Spain, Portugal and Italy.[52] Through the long years of the Spanish conflict, in the last two decades of the sixteenth century, commercial ties with France became increasingly important and a longstanding trade was continued with the Irish ports. Trade with South Wales was also substantial and by the 1620s three local sailors, resident in Heanton Punchardon, were regarded as being engaged only in that for coal.[53] There was also spectacular wealth made from privateering in the 1580s and 1590s. The parish register shows that there was a great range of occupations in the town including tucker, dyer, fuller, glover, cardmaker, potter, netter, roper, lantern-maker, bellman, vintner, surgeon, shipwright, hellier, carrier, fiddler, printer, brick-maker and salt-maker.

The town's population reflected the mercantile interests in the Americas and Africa providing a racial diversity which albeit limited was possibly moderately more varied than it is today. The parish registers provide intriguing evidence of this. In addition to the many Blackmoores[54] there were at least three African servants then living in Barnstaple: in the parish register were recorded the burials of Grace, 'a neiger servant' of Mr Richard Dodderidge on 6 April 1596, Peter Mingus, a 'negor servant' of Mr Norrishe in the following month and in 1605 an un-named 'negro servant' of Mrs Ayer.[55] Dodderidge was a member of the English Guinea Company,[56] which had a monopoly of trade on the Senegal and Gambia, and presumably Grace was brought from there. Mr Norrishe was presumably John Norris who served as one of the town's Members for Parliament and who Wyatt recorded in 1589 as a privateer. His servant Peter Mingus may well have been taken from a prize ship. Unfortunately there is no further information as to whether these three were treated as household servants and given a wage, or considered as their masters' personal property. In addition there was at least one Portuguese, James 'Rodigoo', probably Rodrigues, resident in Barnstaple during the 1570s.[57] The trade connection with Spain is also shown by the later death of Thomas Haukes, a trading agent who resided and died in San Sebastian but was brought back to Barnstaple for his burial.[58] Finally, some residents of north Devon would have seen a more unusual sight: in nearby Bideford lived

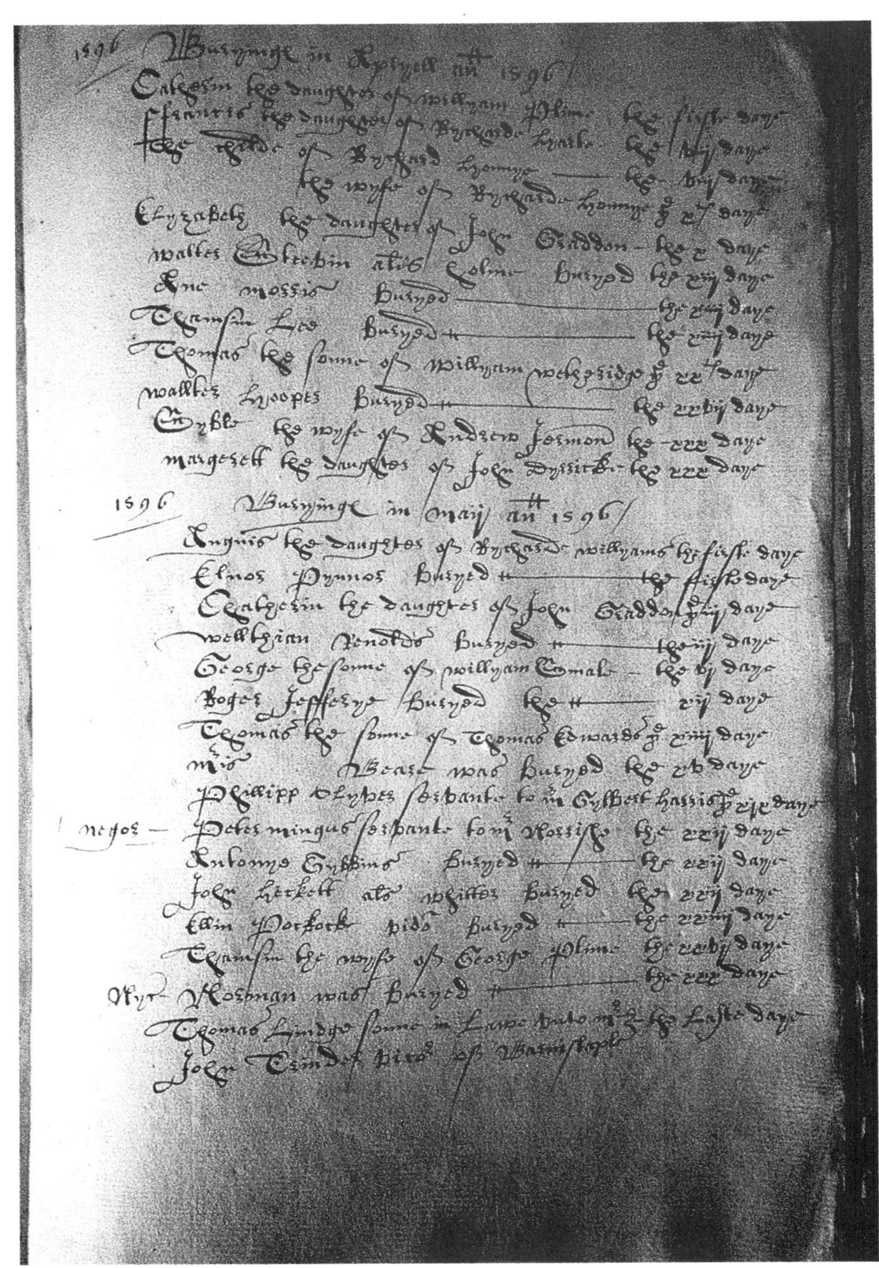

Figure 7. Note of the burial of Peter Mingus, 'negor' servant, in Barnstaple parish register, 1596.

in the late 1580s a native American, christened Raleigh, from Wynganditoia (Wyngandacoia[59] otherwise Virginia). Kingsley described him as a 'free forest wanderer' who was a 'sort of emblem of the sad fate of that worn-out Red Race to whom Civilisation came too late to save'. Presumably Raleigh was also familiar with Barnstaple.[60]

Despite being north Devon's chief commercial centre, Barnstaple was, and remains, distant from Devon's greatest concentration of population and the journey from Exeter to Barnstaple was a full day's ride.[61]

Figure 8. Detail from the coat of arms of John Hawkins showing a young slave girl, 1566.

Figure 9. Detail of decorative woodwork of the Dodderidge overmantel now in Barnstaple Guildhall, early seventeenth century.

Figure 10. Plaster ceiling in the home of an unknown merchant, 62 Boutport Street, drawn by H.H. Sharland.

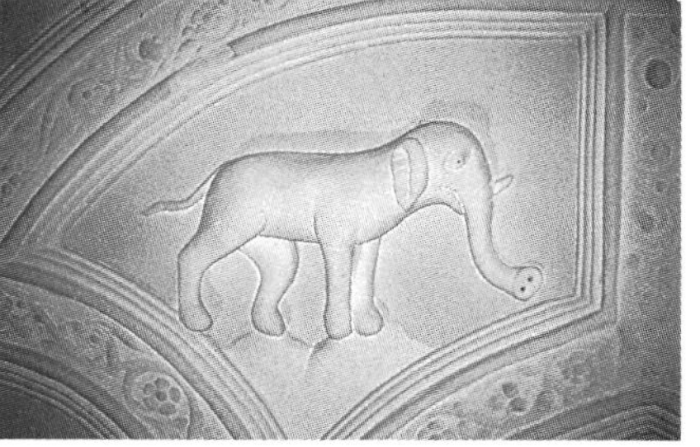

Detail of the decorative plasterwork, 62 Boutport Street, featuring a pair of elephants, early seventeenth century.

Above Left: Detail of the decorative plasterwork, 62 Boutport Street, featuring a heron, early seventeenth century.

Above: Arms of the Spanish Company, dissolved in 1606, in the decorative plasterwork, 62 Boutport Street, early seventeenth century.

Detail of the decorative plasterwork, 62 Boutport Street, featuring Barnstaple Town Arms, early seventeenth century.

It was on neither of the two roads leading from Exeter to the west but it was on the way to Ireland and the Chronicle recorded attempts to improve greater communications to Ireland through the port of Barnstaple. In 1603 a footpost was established to Exeter for letters to London because of the 'great inconveniences which divers times happens and how prejudicial it is many times' to those in north Devon. Every Tuesday morning at seven the post left Barnstaple for Exeter for the fee of six pence for a single letter and eight pence for a 'double' letter. The courier then waited for the London post in order to return to Barnstaple on either Friday night or Saturday morning.[62]

In the middle of the sixteenth century the town, like Exeter before it, sought and gained greater control over its own affairs. In the 1550s and 1560s it was successful in removing two obstacles to greater self-rule. The first achievement came in 1557 when Queen Mary granted a charter of incorporation allowing ownership of land and creation of byelaws. The second objective was to acquire manorial rights which included the fair and markets as well as land rights, notably those of the river bank and the quay. The town appears to have been unable to pay the £420 asking price to the owner, a Warwickshire gentleman, who in 1565 sold it to Sir John Chichester of Raleigh. Within a year it was resold to the corporation, at a profit of one hundred pounds to Sir John. There were some conditions, including that Chichester remained titled Lord of the Manor and retained the nomination of one Member of Parliament.[63]

Figure 11. The Barnstaple ballot pots in the Museum of North Devon.

New charters followed in 1595 and 1609. In 1585, shortly before Wyatt became a town official, new procedures were agreed for electing the mayor and the other officers. The mayor was chosen from a choice of two men from the Common Council. Each member were given a small ball, the candidates' names were written on one of two pots, instructions were given to discreetly place a hand into each pot and then secretly drop the ball. The town's 'ballot pots' are housed today in the Museum of North Devon. The ordinance or byelaw stated that its ancient 'orders, rules and customs' had not been as rigorously followed as needed and that the town had 'fallen into great ruin and decay'. It also noted that recently affairs were being put into proper order.[64] The charter of 1595 brought a new development. Wyatt proudly noted:

> On Monday being the 3rd of May by virtue of the new charter of the liberties of this town, there was kept at the Guildhall a Sessions being the first that ever was kept within this town.

Through strenuous effort and imagination Barnstaple achieved a strong position in order to run its own affairs.

Figure 12. An early seventeenth-century clerk (after a woodcut from *The Constancy of Susanna*, a ballad printed as a pamphlet in 1605).

Adam Wyatt

Adam Wyatt's family came from the nearby parish of Braunton, some eight miles from Barnstaple. He was born in 1548 and had eight siblings, one of whom died an infant. On 27 August 1576, at the age of 28, he married Elizabeth, the daughter of Gilbert Harris of Barnstaple. In total they had ten children, five daughters (Mary, Susan, Frances, Johan and Wilmot) and five sons (George, Nicholas, John, Robert and Adam), who were born either at Braunton or Barnstaple.

The decision to use the spelling 'Wyatt' has been made for uniformity. In the Braunton parish register he was referred to as 'Wyatt' and once as 'Wyott' but in the Barnstaple register, including his burial entry, it was 'Wyot'. On one document in 1591 he signed his name both 'Wyote' and 'Wyate' and on another of the same year he wrote 'Wyote' while his brother signed as 'Wyot' and another close relation, probably either his father or brother, wrote 'Wyotte'. His father was referred to in the parish register as 'Wyott'.[65]

Figure 13. Signatures of Adam Wyatt.

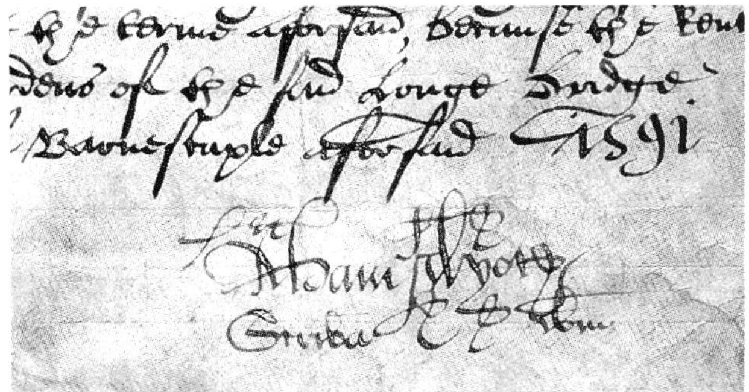

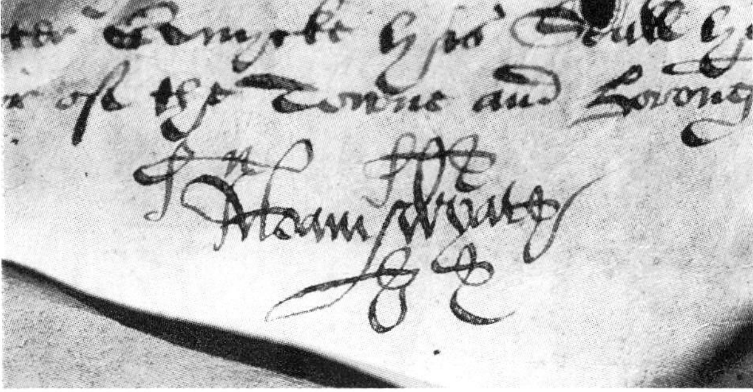

Wyatt was appointed town clerk in 1586 and he remained in Barnstaple for twenty-five years until his death in October 1611.[66] It is probable that he lived somewhere near modern-day Tuly Street given that he leased a stable near St Tuly's Well in 1592.[67] Given that Palmer's copy is now housed there in the North Devon Record Office this is a highly appropriate location. In the Chronicle Wyatt mentions his own family: among the references are to his father's death in 1592[68] and he also referred to his brothers George, Nicholas and Hugh. There is no mention of his wife or children.

Wyatt was employed not only as town clerk but also as steward. The responsibilities were defined by an oath and his early seventeenth century counterparts undertook to:

> well and truly serve our Sovereign Lord the King and also Mr Mayor Aldermen and Burgesses of this Borough and parish of Barnstaple in the office of Steward, Town Clerk, and Clerk of the Peace of the same borough and parish, truly to enter as well all precepts, actions, pleas & processes between party and party in the King's majesty's courts holden before Mr Mayor, the Recorder, Deputy Recorder and Aldermen of this borough and parish of Barnstaple or any of them and also all indictments, presentments, recognizances and other processes in the Sessions of the Peace of our Sovereign Lord the King holden before his Majesty's justices of the peace in the said Borough our parish; when I shall be reasonably requested so to do; by any person or persons or appertaining to my said offices taking therefore not above the due and ordinary fees for the same; and extract or cause to be extracted the perquisites issues, fines and amercements of the same his Majesty's courts and sessions once or twice every year as I shall be commanded by Mr Mayor so to do; and the same to deliver or cause to be delivered unto the Receiver there for the time being for gathering and receiving thereof. And all other things appertaining to my said offices diligently and truly to do and accomplish after the best of my knowledge and as near as God shall lead my conscience, so help me God and his holy Evangelist.[69]

Wyatt received twenty shillings annually from the town for his fee and sixteen pence for 'keeping of the tolsel at the time of the Fair'.[70] This latter sum was for keeping the borough court during Barnstaple Fair (the 'tolsel') which took place in the beginning of September.[71] The fees specified under Wyatt's oath brought in the greatest portion of his income and this explains his resentment at losing the town seal to the mayor in 1608.

The town council comprised the mayor, a senior alderman, junior alderman and twenty-two capital burgesses who were served by some forty local officials. The officers were a recorder, deputy recorder, two coroners, clerk of the market, chamberlain, receiver, several constables, two collectors of the rents, two bailiffs, a first and second sergeant at mace, four searchers of the market and two wardens of Long Bridge. There were also water bailiffs, a pound keeper, scavenger of Long Bridge and of the market, supervisor of the Strangers, two inspectors of weights, two sealers of hides and one bellman.[72] Wyatt's predecessor was called the town's seneschal whereas the term seems to have become modernized at Wyatt's appointment as steward. As his oath shows, he was responsible for the legal running of the borough. The Wyatt family was legally orientated: several were members of the Inner Temple, including his brothers George and Hugh, and others served as an archdeaconry official and Admiralty judge. In 1588 his brother George became treasurer of the Inner Temple. In contrast Adam appears to have achieved success only in Barnstaple.[73]

The Contents of the Chronicle

It is useful to remember that Wyatt's main intention in writing the Chronicle was to record information which he deemed important for the officers of the borough to subsequently refer to. He was interested in listing mayors and other officials, observing remarkable or noteworthy occurrences, particularly relating to weather and the natural world, and charitable bequests[74] but the tone of the work is one of concern for Barnstaple's general well-being. Wyatt noted a wide range of subjects, many related to a town clerk's concerns of good government, for example of one change he wrote 'this order hath no father to any man's remembrance now living, but sprung up of the infected air lately amongst us'. Likewise in 1600 Wyatt disapproved of a dispute between the town council and the vicar: he noted 'there is no likelihood of good government while such dissensions last'.

Unlike other chroniclers there is little in the Barnstaple Chronicle, at least in that part which has survived, relating to the grotesque. Whereas other writers were fascinated by unusual events in the natural world such as monstrous births and human defects[75] Wyatt observed only the unhappy birth in 1601 of a set of twins, one of whom was born dead three days after the first birth.

Wyatt was mindful of maintaining social control and thus watchful of possible threats to orderly conduct such as the trade depression in the 1580s which generated great public unrest. Many entries are concerned with events central to his every-day duties as town clerk, including the arrival of assize judges and other notable persons and of civic occasions. There are numerous references to William, third earl of Bath, and his wife Frances, countess of Bath, but this is expected given that family's importance to north Devon as great landowners, to the

Figure 14. Standing wall-monument of William Bourchier, third earl of Bath, 1623, in Tawstock parish church.

county given that the earl was Lord Lieutenant and particularly to Barnstaple as the town's Recorder. They were also close neighbours; the earl and countess resided only a few miles upriver on the Taw and within sight of Barnstaple.[76] Their home at Tawstock was described by John Hooker as:

> a very famous and an ancient house ... which the said earl doth continually keep in most bountiful order, to his great honour and to the great good of the country and to the relief of the poor.[77]

Some of Wyatt's entries merely note the Bourchiers' deaths and births but most are to the earl's activities as a justice of the peace, concerning such issues as defence, establishing a house of correction, supplying provisions for the navy or overseeing grain prices in the local market. Among the earl's affairs which were of particular concern to local government was his work as Vice Admiral of North Devon. He convened at least one court in the town and Wyatt was suspicious of the motives for this. Two issues concerned Wyatt and the town greatly; the earl claimed the right to elect one of Barnstaple's two members of parliament and to be the town's recorder. The Chichesters chose the other representative to Parliament.

Wyatt had a personal interest in the Bourchier family. His sister-in-law was the earl's aunt: his brother Hugh had married Lady Mary Bourchier, daughter of the second earl of Bath. Several members of the Wyatt family were later senior members of the fifth earl's household, including Thomas who was employed as secretary.[78]

The Chronicle reflects Barnstaple's role in overseas commerce with one reference to Sir Richard Grenville and the colony at Virginia. Wyatt noted that Grenville had 'pretended' to return to the Virginia colony of Roanoke where he had been the previous year.[79] There are observations on the temporary losses of the Newfoundland fishery in 1593 and 1595 and, more importantly, a note in 1603 that local ships had resumed their trade with Spain and Portugal 'as usual'. The first passage in the Chronicle is concerned with the spread of disease from a group of Portuguese prisoners brought back from Newfoundland.[80] Wyatt noted in 1596 that Barnstaple participated in a survey of mariners and shipping but the report appears to have been subsequently

Figure 15. Detail of monument of William Bourchier, 1623, in Tawstock parish church.

Figure 16. Wall monument of Thomas Hinson, servant to the Earl of Bath and Member of Parliament, in Tawstock parish church, 1614.

lost. An earlier survey, of 1572, shows there were then 12 vessels, two of which were between 60 and 100 tons in size and the remainder under 60 tons.[81]

Civic occasions feature prominently. For instance, when in 1587 the earl and countess of Bath dined with the mayor it was archly noted that for the first time the aldermen's wives were excluded and that 'there was much chattering among them'. In 1598, during Innocents' Week, the mayor and other town officials visited the Chichesters at Youlston 'and carried ... some good Handsel'. These goodwill gifts for the New Year were also brought to the Basset family and to the Bourchiers at Tawstock. Some were light-hearted events: he noted the arrival at Ilfracombe on 1 August 1590 of Richard Ferris, a Londoner, who together with several companions, rowed a wherry boat from the Thames to Bristol and then crossed by land with the boat on their return journey to London. In his published account, *The most dangerous and memorable adventure of Richard Ferris*, it is clear that Barnstaple's position upriver was too inconvenient to merit deviating from their journey to Bristol.[82]

More significant is Wyatt's record of the new charter in 1595. He wrote:

> 12th December John Norrys, a burgess of this town, brought a new charter to town which I read in English before the Mayor and most part of the common council.

He was paid nearly two pounds for copying the charter and for 'other work'.[83] The following spring Wyatt duly noted:

> a sessions held at the Guildhall the first after the new charter and the first ever kept in the town.

In 1609 a new charter presented further difficulties when the earl of Bath again insisted upon being given the position of the town's Recorder as he had been in 1596.[84]

It is not surprising that the Guildhall was a continual focus for Wyatt: he duly recorded the attendance there of judges for various

Figure 17. The Old Guildhall by and after E.H. Buckler, *c.*1850.

Figure 18. Detail of the old guildhall woodwork now in the Museum of North Devon.

civic and legal occasions and also noted the repairs and rebuilding of the Guildhall itself as well as of ancillary buildings around it.[85] The Chronicle reflects Wyatt's official legal duties: there are recurrent references to county quarter sessions, the assizes and the borough's many legal cases. The borough records show that he was paid for drawing up legal papers, particularly from 1604 to 1605 and occasionally he was sent to Exeter for legal business.[86] The number and length of some entries must be seen within the context of Wyatt's day-to-day responsibilities.

There are many references to the holding of the assizes at Exeter, Honiton, Tavistock and Barnstaple. Executions were noted, including of eighteen prisoners on the Castle Green at Barnstaple when the court was moved from Exeter because of plague. These included Ulalia Page of Plymouth, who was accused of murdering her husband in 1592. She and her lover, a mariner by the name of George Strangwidge, were made notorious through the pamphlet *The Lamentable Tragedy of Page of Plymouth* and a play *The Merchant of Plymouth* written by Ben Jonson and Thomas Dekker. They were convicted of strangling the Plymouth merchant and both were executed at Barnstaple.[87] It was claimed that Ulalia had been forced to marry against her will and in one version of the play her father concluded:

> Ye rigid parents learn from her sad fate
> Never to wed your children where they hate;
> But if chaste passion their young hearts inspire
> With kind indulgence feed the kindled fire!
> For, if by force the bride and bridegroom led,
> Eternal discord waits the nuptial bed.
> Love should be free; it cannot be contained.
> Nor ever bought or sold; it must be gained.[88]

Crime was a frequent topic: three women were publicly humiliated for their 'filthy and lascivious lives' by being carted through the town and then placed in the stocks. The three women each had an illegitimate child born a few years before and the father of one of the woman may have been carted ten years before as well as the maid-servant of the father of another of the women.[89] Wyatt's note is not as severe as the final epitaph to Eleanor Pattrick who was recorded in the burial register as 'a whore of fame'.[90] Wyatt also noted that one prisoner at Exeter had his ears cut off, his nose slit and the letter 'S' burnt in his face. Occasionally there are references to the proper allocation of public money, a traditional concern of local government and town clerks

Figure 19. 'Punishment at the Exeter assizes' by Mathew Burtnyk, Year 7, Park Community School, Barnstaple, 1998.

Figure 20. 'The execution of eighteen prisoners on the Castle Green' by Jack Steadman, Year 8, Park Community School, Barnstaple, 1998.

Figure 21. 'Punishment of three women at High Cross' by Emma Westcott, Year 8, Park Community School, Barnstaple, 1998.

in particular: when in 1593 chimes were added to the new bell, Wyatt noted it as 'a great charge to small effect'. Equally important to Wyatt was the election of the town's mayors, coroners, clerks of the market and members for parliament. But, as can be seen in the Chronicle, his commentary was not always flattering.

Public Defence

Defence was an issue of recurrent concern to Wyatt: the long conflict with Spain, Irish insurrection and threats from Catholics were all noted by the town clerk as was the organization of local musters, of men, arms and horses. The earl of Bath played a particular part in this.[91] Barnstaple was a port of embarkation for Ireland and Wyatt carefully observed the passing of many hundreds of soldiers through the town. Beacons were another concern, particularly when lightning accidentally lit one nearby beacon.

The Spanish threat was the greatest of the military concerns; Wyatt wrote that either he personally or the town in general was 'much afraid of a Spanish invasion'. In 1587 it was the cause of civil unrest. He wrote:

> this country is daily further charged with ammunition and harness, expecting and providing for invasions and wars which make the common sort fall into poverty for want of trade, so that divers fall to robbing, and stealing, the like hath never been seen.

In 1595 there was a report that several Spanish ships were in the Bristol Channel. The Privy Council ordered the Mayor to send a ship to 'recounter' with them.

Perhaps Wyatt's most well-known entry is that 'five ships went over the bar to join Sr Francis Drake at Plymouth'. Unfortunately Hanmer's copy has no additional information to support that these ships did sail against the Armada. It does however have further, albeit well-known, details on Sir Richard Grenville's later fight on the *Revenge* and shows how prominent the event was within north Devon. Of particular interest are the additional details on the arrival of the *Prudence* from a privateering voyage from Guinea with a Portuguese ship, the *Holy Spirit* of Lisbon.[92] It returned with four chests of gold, which weighed 320 pounds and were valued at £16,000, together with gold chains, civet, ambergris and ivory. Hanmer's copy shows the ship was first brought into Appledore and then taken on the third day to Barnstaple. Wyatt noted that the gold chains were pillaged by the crew. The *Prudence* was one of several privateers which Wyatt observed and he made in total thirteen references to privateering, one concerned a rumour of a rich prize ship brought into a south coast port. As with many other expeditions, Wyatt observed the goods with a certain amount of avarice. The cargoes of these vessels, whether hides, sugar, ginger, cochineal, oils, ivory or bullion, were of great interest to him.

Religion and the Rise of Factions

Wyatt often noted religious affairs and this could have been problematic, or at least awkward, given his position as an employee of the town and the annual turnover in individuals as mayor. In one instance he wrote without any ambiguity 'I am not of their mind'. There is no other evidence relating to Wyatt's religious inclinations although a distant relation was associated with puritanism shortly afterwards.[93] In 1589 Wyatt recorded that John Clarys, vicar of Barnstaple, was excommunicated although there does not appear to be any corrobative evidence in the diocesan records. He died the following year. Wyatt observed that the internal walls of parish church were painted in 1592 and parts of the scriptures were written on the pillars. In August 1595 Barnstaple received an official visitation from the bishop but Wyatt noted that his trip was at best only partially successful. Bishop Babington was greeted at his arrival in South Gate Street by the Mayor and the council in their scarlet gowns, a scholar made a speech, there was dinner with the mayor and afterwards the bishop confirmed 'divers' children in the open air at the Castle Green. It was canonically required of bishops to visit their dioceses and Babbington's successors duly toured the diocese of Exeter.[94] However, Wyatt archly noted:

> on the second day such a multitude came in from the country that he could scarce pass the street, on a sudden he turned up Crock [Cross]

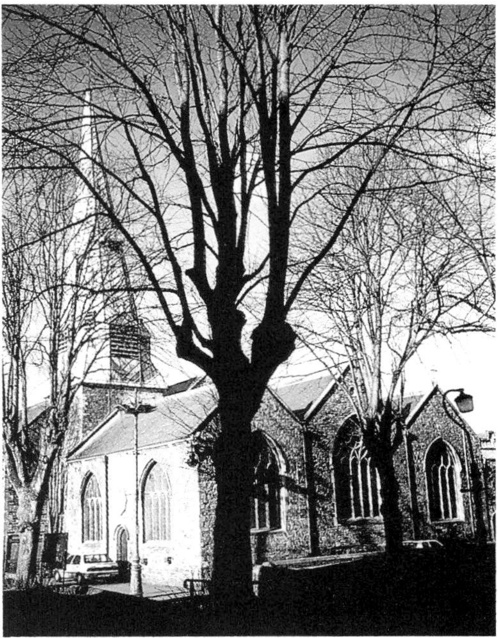

Figure 22. Church of SS Peter and Mary Magdalene, Barnstaple.

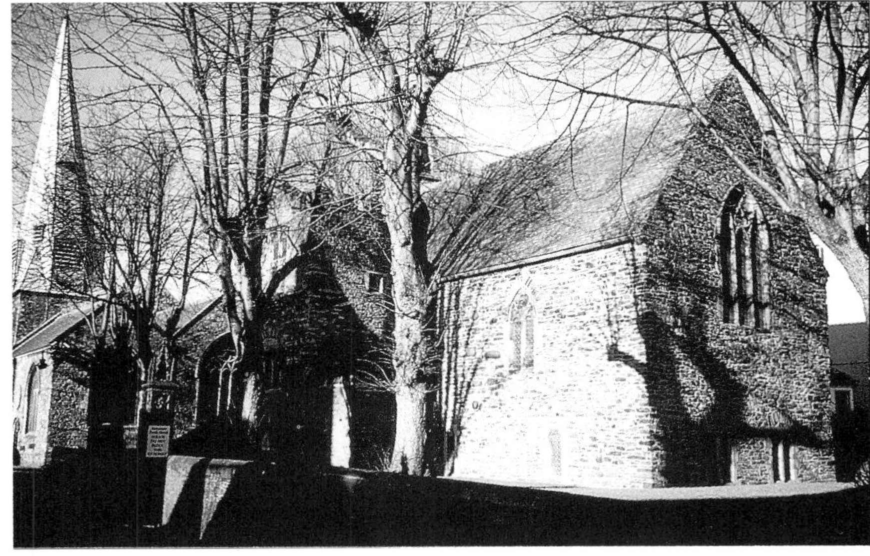

Figure 23. St Anne's Chapel, Barnstaple.

> Street & went to his lodgings, and went out of town almost forthhence. The people lamented they had lost a fine harvest day.

The general population seemingly felt the bishop had let them down and he in turn was apparently overwhelmed by the press of people. This was not unusual: other bishops complained of physical exhaustion from ministering to the crowds. Visitations were popular occasions; another bishop later wrote that after confirming many hundreds 'I nearly melted away with the heat and did indeed earn the right to go to bed' and yet one more also fled to his bed in order to escape the heavy demands. A later bishop of Exeter wrote of the 'fervour and violence of desire that people were wont to sue for this sacred ceremony'. Bishop John Hall claimed:

> How have we been tired with the importunity of suitors impatient of either denial or delay! How have we been oppressed with the throngs of the multitude, striving for the first admission! Insomuch, as we have been forced to call for the help of officers to our rescue from that well-meant impetuousness'.[95]

Confirmation, or 'Bishoping' as it was also known, was intended for those who were carefully prepared by the parish clergy and was the sole formal occasion in which bishops stepped into the laity's spiritual lives.[96] The response at Barnstaple may have been due to Babington's reputation as an effective preacher; he was formerly a city lecturer and was later praised for his 'painful preaching'.[97]

By the end of the sixteenth century Barnstaple had gained a reputation for 'puritanism'. The earl of Bath for one claimed there were 'seditious schismatics' in the town.[98] Not only is this supported by several references throughout the Chronicle but Wyatt appears to show his personal disapproval of them. In one instance Wyatt noted that the town's preacher was denied a licence over his refusal to wear a surplice. He also observed that on 29 April 1599 a schoolmaster brought a child to be baptized to the parish church. He asked for the boy to be called 'Do Well', after what was explained as the Hebrew name 'Abdeel', but the vicar refused and substituted the name John. Wyatt declared that the schoolmaster was 'not very hardly witted but one of the Anabaptistical and precise brethren'. The parish register duly recorded the baptism of John, son of John Symons junior, for that date. But curiously it also recorded that some fourteen years previously another child, the son of Robert Cornval, had been christened 'Abdiel'.[99] There is also another baptism for a child called 'Lovewell' along with many examples of Old Testament names. Ben Jonson parodied the 'puritan' favouring for symbolic first-names with 'Tribulation Wholesome' and 'Win-the-fight Littlewit'[100] and there is one register entry which undoubtedly reflects this practice: on 23 June 1630 The-Lord's-Neare Leakie married John Knell. William Camden specifically questioned in print the origins of the name 'The-Lord's-near'[101] and such naming was criticized as an device to distinquish themselves from the wider community. Another interesting baptism was that for 'Godheard' Asser.[102] There were other unusual names: perhaps the most patriotic occurs for February of 1595 with the christening of a baby girl as 'Armeda' at Barnstaple.

Of particular interest is Wyatt's note of a 'trental of sermons' on 18 and 19 October 1586 at nearby Pilton and Shirwell. A considerable number of men and women rode to attend 'an exercise or holy fast and there some offered [money] as they did when they went on pilgrimage'. Wyatt observed that the thirty sermons were 'to the admiration of all Protestants'. The choice of these places is interesting given that they are immediately outside the town's jurisdiction but presumably organized there in order to take advantage of Barnstaple's regional position. Pilton is particularly interesting as there had been a popular shrine there before the Reformation. It is difficult to assess Wyatt's view of the two events, he may have been sincere in his praise.[103]

The lecturer at Pilton may have been influenced by John Rutherford who not long before this was lecturing there: the bishop of Exeter was informed by a supporter that Rutherford had been sharply reproved:

> for preaching against Bishop Juell but he has cleared himself by the testimony of those of the parish of Pilton that heard him and showed the testimony of the gentlemen of the shire of his pains of preaching and catechism and of his good life and conversation.

It was also requested that Rutherford be allowed to preach at Barnstaple.[104] It was at this time that John Farmer, curate at Barnstaple, wrote of:

> such tumults and frivolous opinions as by their innovations are already bred in the people's hearts. Whereby not only the people of the said town, but also of the country near adjacent, are divided and distracted into sundry opinions and strange conceits, unreverently using the ministers and ministry.[105]

It was also at this time that a dispute broke out between the curate and Eusebius Paget, preacher of Barnstaple, because the latter insisted upon administering only four communions a year. Paget was removed just as Wyatt was appointed town clerk.[106]

Curiously, both Juell and Thomas Harding were former pupils of Barnstaple Grammar School. William Camden noted in 1590 that 'out of this town's school there issued two right learned men and most renowned divines ... who most hotly contended and wrote learnedly the one against the other concerning the truth of religion'.[107] Both were prominent exiles: Juell during the reign of Mary I and subsequently Harding during Elizabeth's reign. Wyatt also made many references to the Dodderidge family, a prominent merchant family whose most famous member was Sir John. He was another former pupil of the school who became justice of the King's bench and wrote *The English Lawyer* and *A Compleat Parson*. A later family member left the Dodderidge Library, a substantial collection of mainly religious volumes which is now housed at the Main Library in the University of Exeter.

It is against this background of increasing religious division or polarization within Barnstaple that Wyatt noted the mayor finding the town's vicar in an alehouse run by one John Williams, just possibly the Jolly Butcher which was a well-known establishment located on the High Street and adjoining the old Guildhall.[108] At nine o'clock on the night of 14 November 1600 John Delbridge, newly elected Mayor, and his two aldermen discovered John Trender with a group of other men playing a drum and pipe and the vicar refused the mayor's order to leave the building. This was the start of a long and serious dispute: Trender was taken into custody, complained to the bishop, the earl of

Bath intervened on his behalf and the mayor was forced to go to Tawstock and release the vicar. The following day, on Sunday, Wyatt critically noted that the vicar preached for two hours and 'being a cold day he wearied all his audience'. Two days later it was determined that there was just cause for legal action against Trender and in January Trender was forced by the mayor and other townsmen to go to the ecclesiastical court. The outcome is unknown but Trender remained vicar of Barnstaple. It has been suggested that the bringing of charges against Trender was a retaliation for the suspension of Richard Smyth who was Barnstaple's preacher and author of *A Munition against Man's Misery and Mortality; a treatice containing the most effectual remedies against the miserable state of man in this life.*[109] The accusers may have been friends of Smyth and among those who called for a replacement following Smyth's death in 1611 was John Delbridge.[110] Trender was in office for almost the whole of Wyatt's term as town office and in 1595 was elected rural dean of the deanery of Barnstaple.[111]

It should also be pointed out that only four years before Trender had already come into conflict with the town. Wyatt observed that during a sermon Trender had compared the aldermen with oxen: he complained that the two men had been absent from church and 'like two fat Oxen that they would not hear when Christ called unto them but drew backwards and drew others from Christ'. Trender was called before the town officials but the earl of Bath intervened on his behalf and ordered the aldermen to be brought before him.

It is possible that Trender's difficulties arose from an increasing intolerance by the 'puritan' elite aimed at the sitting incumbent but Wyatt's presumably more moderate stance indicates that Trender may not have been a particularly able cleric. One historian thought that his 'general unworthiness gave his Puritan critics a useful target in their public argumentation'.[112] Two further legal cases in the church courts involving Trender provide additional insights into his character and the general situation surrounding him. At about this time he brought a suit of defamation against a neighbour, John Davy, whose words were to the 'derogation of his calling'. Davy claimed, among other things, that Trender was a 'lying varlet'.[113] However, the second case, brought by Trender's own wife, has details which challenge the view that the vicar was being unfairly harassed by a 'puritan' oligarchy. The dispute concerned cruelty and non-maintenance and partly centred around the occupancy of the vicarage, a building which after Trender's residence was described as having some thirteen rooms and being built of stone and cob and faced with Cornish slate.[114] In 1607 Joan Trender argued before the court that her husband refused to adequately provide for her, having driven her from the vicarage. In his own defence the vicar claimed to have considered his wife to be:

> a drunkard and the most notorious drunkard that is in the whole country and that also she is a whore and that he will see her hanged and damned before he will have her home to his home or mutual security.

He had asserted that she hid 'knaves under his bed that by his wife's appointment lay in wait or were there to kill him'. She was also claimed to have called her mother-in-law 'filth', Judas and Satan.[115] But the accusations against Trender were not only that he refused to support his wife but also that he was a violent man and had threatened to kill her. One Barnstaple resident, Joan Lugg, testified that some ten years previously she was in Bath with her husband and the vicar and his wife. They shared the same bedroom and slept in a trundle bed while the Trenders were in the 'high bed'. In the middle of the night she heard Trender cry out 'thou beast, I will make thee be quiet ... I never be at rest for thee' whereupon he struck the bedpost with a sword. On another occasion it was claimed that Trender threw burning coals from a warming pan at his wife and on another instance she was struck by a brass candlestick which had a candle burning in it. She cut her face and lost a tooth. It was alleged he threatened to 'make an end of her'. Finally, it was related that in the vicarage one evening he 'barbarously' beat her with an iron curtain rod until she was 'black and blue'.

The testimony of John Delbridge is particularly interesting and relevant. He related that seven years before, at the time when Delbridge found Trender in the alehouse, Mrs Trender had complained of her husband's temper and treatment of her but that she was then unwilling to testify and Delbridge was thus unable to proceed with a case against the vicar.[116] Trender remained in office until his death in 1628 whereupon Delbridge successfully petitioned the bishop for Martin Blake, Delbridge's son-in-law, to be given Trender's place.[117] The inscription on Trender's memorial stone in Barnstaple parish church proclaims 'Many are the troubles of the righteous, but the Lord delivereth them out of all'.

John Delbridge had a significant role in these disputes with Trender. Delbridge, a leading merchant, twice mayor and Member of Parliament for Barnstaple, was also in contention with the third earl of Bath who in 1601 referred to him as 'a factious pernicious head' of the Barnstaple 'schismatics'. Furthermore, Delbridge chose as his wife Agnes Downe, niece of the afore-mentioned Bishop John Juell.[118] It must have been in relation to Trender's alehouse visit that in June 1602 Delbridge thanked the earl of Salisbury for his support and mediation with the earl of Bath.[119] It does not appear to have reconciled the earl and Delbridge to any lasting degree. Only a few years later there was yet another dispute between the two men; during the summer of 1606, Bath declared to Salisbury that Delbridge was:

> the secrett of all this busines, my good Lo: and of your Lps trouble and my disgrace therin, resteth wholie in your lps servaunt John Delbridge ... who gloryeth in his opposicon wth me in manie things els ... hath of late yeares diverslie wronged and dishonared me.[120]

The two men had clashed over the arrest of John Sweet, a traveller suspected of being a recusant, who was discovered in Barnstaple. Delbridge had the man arrested on the instructions of the earl of Salisbury but enraged the earl of Bath by refusing to release Sweet to him. In turn the earl of Salisbury reprimanded Bath for attempting to override the Privy Council's authority and advised:

> in such a case your Lo[rdshi]p shall do well to forbeare to intermeddle with them, least out of yor affection to do servic you may disorder servic. for my Lord, yow have no other power to deale in such cases as you are a Lieutenant then Justices of peace

He also asked 'I praie yor Lo[rdshi]p to alter any the least dislike you have of the poor Maior, whom I must needes justifie to have deserved well'. The earl regarded his authority to have been compromised.[121]

It is interesting that once again the clash was over a religious issue; Sweet had travelled to Barnstaple in order to visit the same Lady Bassett whom Wyatt noted had moved that year to the town and was the wife of Sir Robert, a suspected Catholic.[122] Nevertheless, the long cantankerous history between the earl and Delbridge may have become personal even if the original cause was religious. The religious element may have been exacerbated by personal animosity. Yet another dispute shows that the animosity between the two men could also extend to non-religious issues.

The Expansion along the Strand and the Earl of Bath

In 1603 the town officials began upgrading facilities for ships along the Strand. The improvements were partly needed at Barnstaple to accommodate a greater volume and size of vessels in much the same way as other Devon ports, such as Plymouth and Dartmouth, were expanding. The plans resulted in an instant conflict with the earl and the issue dragged on for six years.[123] Wyatt noted in 1603 that work had begun and almost immediately, in June of the following year, he wrote that the earl had started proceedings to have the work stopped in his capacity as Vice Admiral of north Devon. The court declared that the work prejudiced the passage of vessels but the town appealed to the Privy Council and the case was again brought before a court in 1607. The judges inspected the passage of vessels and Wyatt noted that all passed safely with the exception of one sand barge which he suggested deliberately hit the bridge. The issue dominated Wyatt's writing for the following two years until the dispute ended with a dinner provided by the town.[124]

The earl was widely influential and as a great landowner his holdings included a number of manors around Barnstaple. These interests would potentially bring the earl into conflict with a town which was growing increasingly independent. While there are a number of other possibilities, including personal animosity towards Delbridge or possibly

Figure 24. Sketch by G.L. Abbot, 1852, showing the quay, West Gate and the Quay Hall in the Museum of North Devon.

an aversion to the trend towards puritanism within Barnstaple, the mechanism for continual discord with the town's officials was the number of roles which the earl played on a local, regional and national level.

Weather and Harvest Failures

Wyatt was particularly interested in local weather and provides insights into unusual events such as in 1599 when there was 'a violent tempest of wind'. Wyatt noted several periods of extremely cold weather including in September 1593 when the river Taw froze and during the winter of 1607 to 1608 conditions were colder. A note in the parish register recorded weeks of exceptional weather in December 1607 when the river froze and it was possible to walk on the Taw from Long Bridge to the Castle.[125] Wyatt noted that he had to roast his meat a second time, for a full hour and half, before it was warmed straight through. The cold weather also killed many wild birds. The winter was severe across England as well as overseas: the lead pipes froze in Plymouth, the river Thames froze over and the first colonists in New England, many of whom came from Devon, despaired of the extreme cold there and returned home.[126]

Barnstaple had recurrent problems with wind and flooding. At four o'clock in the afternoon of Michaelmas eve in 1586 a westerly wind caused a flood which covered the marshes and then tore the roofs off many buildings. However, on the morning of 20 January 1607 there was a greater flood. Wyatt observed that the tide was five to six feet higher than in living memory and merchandise worth £1,000 was damaged or lost. Among the houses destroyed was that of James Frost who died when the roof fell in as did his two children who were asleep in bed. The deaths are confirmed in the parish register[127] which also certifies that the storm began at three in the morning and continued for nine hours.[128]

The most common weather references concern corn harvests. Society was vulnerable to periodic shortages of grain and Wyatt, as town clerk, was sensitive to the weather's effect on corn prices. Localized weather conditions had a dramatic effect on crop yields and this is repeatedly indicated in his Chronicle. Wyatt was concerned for the general population given that grain formed a significant portion of the general diet. He noted particularly good harvests in 1587, 1588 and especially in 1599 when 'a better harvest never heard of than this'. Wyatt also recorded high grain prices in 1586 to 1587, 1591 and 1595 to 1597. Some prices were caused by the anticipation of a bad harvest, such as followed exceptional rain in the autumn of 1588. Across the country there were bad harvests in 1586, from 1594 to 1597 and again in 1608.[129]

There were several reasons for higher prices. In the spring of 1587 and again in 1590 it was drought, in the summer of 1595 there was exceptional rain and heavy storms and throughout 1596 there was again heavy rain. Rain also caused problems in the summer of 1597 and in 1607 the winter was unseasonably cold.

In 1587 the government issued the Book of Orders to ensure that adequate supplies of grain reached the markets.[130] The market in Barnstaple, then as now, occurred on a Friday and it was generally regarded as a well-attended market with the lowest prices and highest choice of goods in north Devon.[131] Wyatt noted that surveys were made of those who held surplus supplies of grain but these have not survived. In May 1596, during another difficult period, the town official cited a number of bakers and forty brewers and tipplers for acting contrary to the statute.[132]

Provisioning for the Crown occasionally increased both shortages and prices but the main problem appears to have been adverse weather conditions, whether too wet or dry. Measures were undertaken in these years of shortages to increase the supply of grain. A great deal of grain was regularly brought by sea, particularly from 'The Forest', probably the Forest of Dean. However, in 1587 some 700 bushels of rye were brought in 'at the procurement of some of this town'. Nine years later, in the summer of 1596, there was again a great scarcity and dearth. Wyatt wrote that the town needed nothing less than an entire ship's loading of grain and some £1,200 was raised locally. Wyatt noted that 'such snatching and catching for that little and such a cry that the like was never heard'. Prices rose through the year and public money purchased two considerable quantities of rye but prices remained high. In June 1597 three ships returned from Danzig (Gdansk) with rye but the following month the price of wheat peaked at twenty shillings the bushel, a vastly inflated rate of nearly ten-fold. Prices gradually dropped over the following year and in 1599 Wyatt wrote of an exceptionally good harvest.

In 1608 there were again problems with grain shortages and the earl of Bath wrote of the:

> fear of the inconvenience that may ensue by the present dearth of corn and victuals suddenly grown and like more and more to grow in this county if speedy course be not taken to prevent or at least moderate the same. The poorer sort, being the greater number, being already to murmur

> as much and more than they did in the time of the greatest dearth that was and what may ensue thereof is to me somewhat doubtful.[133]

One cause for the shortages was the purchase of grain for use by the overseas fishing fleet either for bread, hard biscuit or for brewing. In that same year Cornish justices claimed that a Barnstaple brewer had created shortages in one part of Cornwall by purchasing 700 bushels of grain. North Devon merchants regularly purchased Cornish grain during times of shortages to supplement their particular needs for the fishing vessels: in 1629 the *Marie* of Braunton carried over 600 bushels of grain from the north Cornish port of Padstow for Barnstaple and two vessels from Northam also carried wheat to Bideford. Four years later, in 1633, the merchants of Barnstaple were forced to agree to purchase over 500 bushels of grain outside the town's market in order to prevent local shortages.[134]

Death and Infectious Disease

Wyatt continually refers to death in his Chronicle. In addition to those already mentioned, he wrote of the attempted suicide of a woman who jumped from Long Bridge[135] but was rescued, and also of a female servant of John Chichester of Marwood who successfully hanged herself 'at the buttery door'. As mentioned earlier Wyatt noted a local woman gave birth to a child and then to another three days later, which was born dead. He provided a fulsome obituary for Clement Burton, former servant and secretary to a local gentleman. He had 'lived a bachelor, he was accounted a wise man and a good scholar and would buy and have the most part of all new books made whereby he had a great library'.

The Chronicle began with a note of the spread of disease from prisoners in the cells at Exeter to the justices. Many died of the 'gaol sickness'. Not surprisingly plague and other infectious diseases were of great concern to a man interested in public order. Wyatt noted rumours of outbreaks in other places (Totnes, Exeter, South Molton, Great Torrington) and in 1591 he observed that watchmen checked

Figure 25. Six-poster monument of Frances, Lady Fitzwarren, 1589, in Tawstock parish church.

Figure 26. Detail of six-poster monument of Frances, Lady Fitzwarren.

travellers suspected of carrying infection. Not surprisingly, the town had a long history of disease; in the 1540s there was a serious outbreak,[136] in 1579–80 at least forty died from plague in Barnstaple and in 1597 there was another period of infectious disease. In 1604 plague again entered the town although curiously Wyatt wrote that few died despite at least 34 deaths were noted elsewhere as occurring from plague, including two children from the 'pest house'.[137] One notable casualty, who died nearby at Tawstock, was the countess of Bath. It may have been merely coincidence, and not some infectious disease, but in 1589 there were five burials of people noted as being particularly old, such as 'the old mother Bowden' and Thomas Norris who was aged 91.[138] The last entry in the Chronicle was written shortly before Wyatt's own death in October 1611.

The Chronicle recorded many extraordinary events, many of which not only add colour but provide unique information on Barnstaple. The main worth of the Chronicle lies in its insights into late Elizabethan and early Stuart society. To the question 'Why at Barnstaple?', originally punned in verse in 1824, the answer must be 'why not?'. The town was a bustling commercial centre with a new-found feeling of self-determination and it is not surprising that Wyatt, as town clerk, exhibited his confidence and civic pride by recording the history he was helping to create.

NOTES

1. John Roberts Chanter, *The Sketches of the Literary History of Barnstaple* (Barnstaple, 1866), 9–10.
2. For example, see R. Pearse Chope, 'New Light on Sir Richard Grenville: The North Devon Fleet against the Armada', *Transactions of the Devonshire Association* XLIX (1917), 260.
3. Bruce W. Oliver, 'The Early Seventeenth-Century Plaster Ceilings of Barnstaple', *Transactions of the Devonshire Association* XLIX (1917), 196.
4. For example, see the enquiry by John Roberts, *Devon & Cornwall Notes & Queries*, XXX (1965), 22.
5. I am grateful to Joyce Youings for this information.
6. N(orth) D(evon) R(ecord) O(ffice), B12/Z1. A later copy, B20/Z1, was deposited on 23 March 1988. The history of the Athenaeum was written by J.R. Chanter, *The Literary Sketches of Barnstaple* (1866) and more recently by Alfred E. Blackwell, 'The North Devon Athenaeum at Barnstaple' XCIII (1961), 174–83. William Palmer senior, and his son William, were mayors of Barnstaple and the reference to being a clerk may be a clerical error. The date 1771 is referred to in the volume in the later notes by Frayne.
7. William Matthews, *British Diaries, 1442–1942* (Berkley, 1942), 4.

8. NDRO, B517/1.
9. Chanter, *Sketches of the Literary History of Barnstaple*, 89–90; NDRO, B12/Z1. I am grateful to Tony Collins for pointing out that Mrs Yeo was the daughter of Mrs Roch.
10. Unfortunately there is no accession file for the manuscript but it is stamped with the date 4 May 1926.
11. Somerset Record Office, SF 4051.
12. Daniel and Samuel Lysons, *Magna Britannia being a Concise Topographical Account of the Several Counties of Great Britain: Volume the sixth containing Devonshire* (1822), 31.
13. Patricia Mcfarland, *A Dynasty of Town Clerks: The Hunt family of Stratford upon Avon* (Dugdale Society Occasional Papers, no.37, 1996).
14. By 1641 another man by the name of Adam Wyatt died 'beyond the seas': Westcountry Studies Library, OM Coll/8/36.
15. Adam Wyatt's father was buried on 23 December 1592, his brother buried 22 August 1608 at Braunton and his nephew baptized 5 August 1586: NDRO, Barnstaple and Braunton parish registers.
16. NDRO, B19z/1, notes on town clerks of Barnstaple.
17. Lois Lamplugh, *Barnstaple, Town on the Taw* (Chichester, 1983), 45.
18. Joyce Youings, 'Some Early Topographers of Devon and Cornwall', in Mark Brayshay (ed.), *Topographical Writers in South-West England* (Exeter, 1996), 52–8.
19. Westcountry Studies Library, Revd J.R. Powell's Notes on Devonshire and Cornwall Parishes (*c*.1870–1900), VII, 397.
20. Chanter termed it a 'local chronicle': Chanter, *Sketches of the Literary History of Barnstaple*, 64.
21. D(evon) R(ecord) O(ffice), ECA/Book 51; M.M. Rowe, 'Seventeenth-Century Exeter Annalists', *Devon & Cornwall Notes & Queries* XXXIII (1974), 20–22; Lieut. Col. Harding, *The History of Tiverton, in the county of Devon* (1845, 1847), two volumes; John J. Beckerlegge, *Plymouth Memoirs, a manuscript by Dr James Yonge* (Plymouth, 1951).
22. Westcountry Studies Library, sxB/TOR 7/0001/DYM, Annals of Torquay and Torbay, 1080–1880, by Robert Dymond, *c*.1880.
23. Alan Dyer, 'English town chronicles', *The Local Historian* vol. 12 no. 6 (May, 1977), 285.
24. For recent work on annals see Rosamond McKitterick, 'Constructing the Past in the Early Middle Ages: the Case of the Royal Frankish Annals', *Transactions of the Royal Historical Society* Sixth series VII (1997), 101–29.
25. J.R. Chanter & Thomas Wainwright (eds), *Reprint of the Barnstaple Records* (Barnstaple, 1900), II, 52; J.R. Chanter, *Sketches of Some Striking Incidents in the History of Barnstaple* (Barnstaple, 1865), 120–22.
26. Susan Reynolds, 'The Forged Charters of Barnstaple', *English Historical Review* LXXXIV (1969), 699.
27. DRO, ECA 51, fo. 236.
28. Samuel Izacke, *Remarkable Antiquities of the City of Exeter* (1723).
29. Harding, *History of Tiverton.*
30. Beckerlegge, *Plymouth Memoirs.*
31. Peter Clark, 'Visions of the Urban Community: Antiquarians and the English City before 1800', in Derek Fraser and Anthony Sutcliffe (eds), *The Pursuit of Urban History* (1983), 111.
32. Clark, 'Visions of the Urban Community', 112; D.R. Woolf, 'Genre into Artifact: the Decline of the English Chronicle in the Sixteenth Century', *The Sixteenth Century Journal* XIX, no.3 (1988), 321. For the history of chronicles also see Rosemary Sweet, *The Writing of Urban Histories in Eighteenth-Century England* (Oxford, 1997), 74–99.
33. Woolf, 'Genre into Artifact', 325. I have taken this term from D.R. Woolf's article.
34. Local examples are William Whiteway of Dorchester and Sir Walter Yonge of Colyton: *William Whiteway of Dorchester; His Diary 1618 to 1635* (Dorset Record Society) XII (1991) & G. Roberts (ed.), *The Diary of Walter Yonge* (Camden Society) OS 41 (1848).
35. Dyer, 'English town chronicles', 286.
36. Jonathan Barry, 'Provincial Town Culture, 1640–80: Urbane or Civic', in Joan H. Pittock and Andrew Wear (eds), *Interpretation and Cultural History* (Basingstoke, 1991), 213.
37. Chanter & Wainwright, *Barnstaple Records*, I, 197.
38. H. Fulford Williams, 'The Hanmer family in North Devon', *Devon & Cornwall Notes & Queries* XXVII, Part VIII (October 1957), 16, 212–15; Rodney Dennys, 'The Hanmer Family in North Devon', *Devon & Cornwall Notes & Queries* XXVII, Part IX (January 1958), 247–8. The copy was made by Revd Jonathan Hanmer (baptized 1606, died 1687), who married Katherine Strange and passed to their third son John Hanmer (baptized 1642, died 1709). He married Jane Parminter in 1683. It passed to their fourth daughter Rebecca (baptized 1686, died 1757) who married Robert Tristram in 1706. It then passed to their sixth daughter Jane who in 1737 married Isaac Welman of Poundsford Park, Taunton, Somerset. At some point it was found at Poundsford Park and acquired by the Sanford Family of Chipley Park near Minehead. It was given by them to the Somerset Record Office on 30 April 1936.
39. Tristram Risdon, *The chorographical description or Survey of the county of Devon* (1811 edn). Risdon wrote of the great flood in 1607 but not only is there no indication he received this information from Wyatt but the account varies considerably in its detail; Thomas Westcote, *A View of Devonshire* (Exeter, 1845 edn).
40. Richard Polwhele, *The History of Devonshire in three volumes* (1793–1806).
41. Lysons, *Magna Brittania: Devon*, 31–4. There are slight differences between the two versions but these may have been clerical or typographical errors.
42. This was volume two.
43. Joseph Besly Gribble, *Memorials of Barnstaple* (Barnstaple, 1830), 618–29.
44. Chanter, *Sketches of Some Striking Incidents*, 87–120.
45. Lysons, *Magna Britannia: Devon*, 31.
46. I am grateful to Dr Jonathan Barry for this information from his forthcoming work on population in Roger Kain and William Ravenhill (eds), *The Historical Atlas of the South West* (Exeter, 1999).
47. Joyce Youings, 'Tudor Barnstaple: New Life for an Ancient Borough', *Transactions of the Devonshire Association*, 121 (1989), 1.
48. Risdon, *Survey of Devon*, 327.
49. Risdon, *Survey of Devon*, 329.
50. Bruce Oliver, 'The Long Bridge of Barnstaple, Part One', *Transactions of the Devonshire Association*, 70 (1938), 194.

51. NDRO, Braunton parish register, burial of 20 November 1578. See also Cornwall Record Office, Padstow parish register, note that six Padstow men were drowned on 11 December 1626 crossing the Bar.
52. Alison Grant, 'Devon Shipping, Trade and Ports, 1600–1689', in Duffy *et al.*, *The New Maritime History of Devon*, I, 130–38. See also Alison Grant, *Atlantic Adventurer, John Delbridge of Barnstaple, 1564–1639* (Instow, 1996) and particularly 'Breaking the Mould: North Devon Maritime Enterprise, 1560–1640', 119–40, in Todd Gray, Margery Rowe and Audrey Erskine (eds), *Tudor and Stuart Devon: The Common Estate and Government* (Exeter, 1992).
53. They were Philip Sander, Geoffrey Stoke and Robert Stoke: Todd Gray (ed.), *Early Stuart Mariners and Shipping* (Devon & Cornwall Record Society), NS 33 (1990), 91.
54. Blackmoore is a longstanding surname in Barnstaple and north Devon.
55. NDRO, Barnstaple parish register, burials of 6 April 1596, 22 May 1596 and 8 July 1605 cited in Alison Grant, 'Breaking the Mould', 127.
56. Grant, *Atlantic Adventurer*, 8.
57. NDRO, Barnstaple parish register, burial 17 November 1574.
58. NDRO, Barnstaple parish register, burial 26 January 1625.
59. David Quinn, *New American World: A Documentary History of North America to 1612* (1979), III, 271, 294.
60. Grant, *Grenville*, 21. He was baptized on 25 March 1588 and was buried on 7 April 1589: NDRO, Bideford parish register. Also, on 15 April 1588 there was buried 'an old French man bound for Terra Virginia'; Alison Grant and Peter Christie, *The Book of Bideford* (Buckingham, 1987), 22.
61. While enroute from Tawstock to Exeter the fifth Earl of Bath generally broke his journey at Bow near Crediton but the journey could be made within a day: Todd Gray (ed.), *Devon Household Accounts, 1627–59: Part Two, Henry, fifth Earl of Bath, and Rachel, Countess of Bath, of Tawstock and London, 1637–1655*, Devon & Cornwall Record Society, NS 39 (1996).
62. Chanter and Wainwright, *Reprint*, II, 215.
63. Youings, 'Tudor Barnstaple', 1–14; Chanter and Wainwright, *Reprint*, II, 255–7.
64. Chanter and Wainwright, *Reprint*, I, 88–9.
65. NDRO, B1/51 and 3704M/TL4/24; Braunton parish register, burial 23 December 1592.
66. The parish register recorded the burial of 'Mr Adam Wyott, town clerk' on 10 October 1611. He was preceded as town clerk and steward by Philip Wyot and replaced by Thomas Davy: NDRO, B1/3972.
67. NDRO, B1/71. I am grateful to Tim Wormleighton for this reference.
68. He was buried on 23 December: NDRO, Braunton parish register.
69. NDRO, Book of Oaths, 10–11. 'Well and' appears to have been crossed through.
70. NDRO, B1/3972, Barnstaple Receiver's Accounts.
71. The date 8 September was kept unless it fell on a Sunday whereupon the Fair was held the following day.
72. Chanter and Wainwright, *Reprint*, I, 45–6, 35–6.
73. Joseph Foster, *Alumni Oxonienses; the members of the Universities of Oxford, 1500–1714* (Oxford, 1891), 1690; NDRO, B1/4/47. His brother George entered in November 1554, was called to the bench in 1574, made reader in 1575, double reader in 1586 and treasurer in 1588. His brother Hugh entered in 1560. Other relations included his nephews Philip who entered in November 1608 and Hugh in November 1611: *Students admitted to the Inner Temple, 1547–1660* (1877), 19, 39, 184 and 196. For discussion of the legal world see Wilfred Prest, 'Lawyers', in Wilfred Prest (ed.), *The Professions in Early Modern England* (1987), 64–89.
74. Sweet, *The Writings of Urban Histories*, 74.
75. Dyer, 'English town chronicles', 290.
76. See James Coulter, *Tawstock and the Lords of Barnstaple* (Bideford, 1996).
77. British Library, Harl.5827, fo. 124d. I would like to thank Professor Joyce Youings for this extract.
78. Gray, *Household Accounts*, 206.
79. David Quinn (ed.), *New American World: A Documentary History of North America to 1612* (1979), III, 283–313.
80. David Quinn, *New American World*, IV, 48–9.
81. M.M. Oppenheim, *The Maritime History of Devon* (1969), 38–40. See also Joyce Youings with Peter W. Cornford, 'Seafaring and Maritime Trade in Sixteenth-Century Devon', in Duffy *et al.*, *The New Maritime History of Devon*, I, 98–107.
82. Richard Ferris, *The Most Dangerous and Memorable Adventures of Richard Ferris* (1590). There were also men called Ferris then resident in Barnstaple.
83. Chanter and Wainwright, *Reprint*, II, 145.
84. This was an issue once more in 1622: Chanter and Wainwright, *Reprint*, II, 13.
85. See Robert Tittler, *Architecture and Power: The Town Hall and the English Urban Community, c.1500–1640* (Oxford, 1991).
86. NDRO, B1/3972/164 & 156.
87. Chanter, *Sketches*, 10–13; Harvey Crane, *Playbill: a history of the theatre in the West Country* (Plymouth and London, 1980), 27–9.
88. Harvey Crane, *Playbill: A history of the theatre in the West Country* (Plymouth, 1980), 29.
89. NDRO, Barnstaple parish register. William son of Anne Keyninges was baptized 6 June 1592, Arthur, son of Marye Davys was baptized 1 April 1593 and Emmet, daughter of Agnes Gayes was baptized 13 June 1593; Chanter and Wainwright, *Reprint*, II, 111.
90. NDRO, Barnstaple parish register, burial of 28 April 1599.
91. Youings, 'Tudor Barnstaple', 1–14.
92. Grant, *Atlantic Adventurer*, 8.
93. John Wyatt (or Wiatt) of Axmouth was accused along with several neighbours of not attending services in the parish church but of attending lectures by puritan preachers. They were also accused of being separatists and one was called 'a most dangerous Anabaptistical fellow': DRO, CC181/34.
94. Bishop William Cotton held visitations in 1600, 1613 and 1616. Bishop Valentine Carey in 1622 and 1625: Fincham, *Prelates as Pastor*, 112, 321. The official visitation books begin in 1622: DRO, records of the diocese of Exeter.
95. Kenneth Fincham, *Prelate as Pastor: The Episcopate of James I* (Oxford, 1990), 128.
96. Fincham, *Prelate as Pastor*, 123–4.
97. Fincham, *Prelate as Pastor*, 88.

98. Roberts, 'Reflections', 142, citing HMC, *Hatfield Mss* XI (188?), xi, 443.
99. NDRO, Barnstaple parish register, 2 June 1585.
100. Nicholas Tyacke, 'Popular Puritan Mentality in Late Elizabethan England', in Peter Clark, Alan G.T. Smith and Nicholas Tyacke (eds), *The English Commonwealth, 1547–1640* (Oxford, 1979), 77.
101. NDRO, Barnstaple parish register, marriage 23 June 1630; Tyacke, 'Popular Puritan Mentality', 78.
102. Grant, *Atlantic Adventurer*, 46–9, 50.
103. Patrick Collinson, 'Elizabethan and Jacobean Puritanism as Forms of Popular Religious Culture', in Christopher Durston and Jacqueline Eales (eds), *The Culture of English Puritanism, 1560–1700* (1996), 53.
104. H(istorical) M(anuscripts) C(ommission), *Calendar of the Manuscripts of the Most Hon. the Marquis of Salisbury*, XIV (1923), 295–6. The letter is undated. Rutherford died in 1577: *The Concise Dictionary of National Biography; From Earliest times to 1985* (Oxford, 1992), 2615.
105. Ian Gowers, 'Puritianism in the County of Devon between 1570 and 1641' (University of Exeter MA thesis, 1970), 40.
106. Gowers, 'Puritanism in the county of Devon', 273–4.
107. Grant, *Atlantic Adventurer*, 6–7.
108. Chanter and Wainwright, *Reprint*, II, 31. The Jolly Butcher was in business until the 1830s: I am grateful to Tim Wormleighton for this information.
109. He may have been the translator of a work by Pierre du Moulin the elder: *British Library Catalogue of Printed Books*.
110. Gowers, 'Puritanism in the county of Devon', 127.
111. DRO, Chanter 784, 25 September 1595.
112. Gowers, 'Puritanism in the county of Devon', 92.
113. DRO, CC15/18.
114. In 1726 it was described as 'half is double-roofed and two stories in height containing eight bays of building, is built with stone and mud walls rough cased excepting the porch in the front which is built with brick. The whole house ic covered with Cornish slates. The number of rooms above and below are thirteen. The kitchen, pantry and hall are floored with lime ashes, the parlour and chamber with deal and the two cellars are pitched with small stones. All the rooms above and below are ceiled and one wainscotted except one side of the hall, kitchen and pantry': DRO, Barnstaple glebe terrier, 2 September 1726. It was not the same as during Trender's residence because after his death the vicarage was rebuilt by Martin Blake: Bridget Cherrry and Nikolaus Pevsner, *The Buildings of England: Devon* (1989), 158.
115. DRO, CC3B/86–7.
116. DRO, CC3A/6, 9, 16, 20 & CC3B/86–7.
117. NDRO, Barnstaple parish register, burials 17 November 1628; DRO, Principal Registry, basket A/1862. Delbridge wrote on 14 September 1628.
118. HMC, *Salisbury* XI, 443; Grant, *Atlantic Adventurer*, 7.
119. Public Record Office, SP12/284/33.
120. Hatfield House, CP117/66v. A modernized version was printed in HMC, *Salisbury*, XVIII, 234–5.
121. Hatfield House, CP117/32. A modernized version was printed in HMC, *Salisbury*, XVIII, 234–5. Delbridge was not the mayor but a leading figure in the town.
122. HMC, *Salisbury* XVIII, 213, 252.
123. See Grant, *Atlantic Adventurer*, 21–4.
124. NDRO, B1/3972/168–77.
125. NDRO, Barnstaple parish register, baptisms, December 1607.
126. David B. Quinn and Alison M. Quinn (eds), *The English New England Voyages, 1602–1608*, Hakluyt Society, second series 161 (1983), 77–90; Todd Gray, 'Devon's Fisheries and Early-Stuart Northern New England', in Michael Duffy *et al.* (eds), *The New Maritime History of Devon*, I, 142.
127. Wainwright, *Reprint*, II, 133–4. In the burials register it was noted 'James Frost, widow, Sabbin and Catherin, his towe daughters, were killed with the fall of his howse, and were buried the 20th of January, 1606 ie 1607 new style, the day of their death'.
128. Wainwright, *Reprint*, II, 134. The baptismal register notes 'in the 20th day of Janiari 1606 there was such a mighte storme and tempeste from the river of Barnstapl with the coming of the tyde that yt caused much loss of goods and houses, to the vallew of towe thowsand pounds, besides the death of one James Froste, a toaker, and two of his children, the which his house fell downe upon them and killed them. This storm began at three o'clock in the morning, and continued till 12 of clock of the same daye'.
129. See Andrew B. Appleby, *Famine in Tudor and Stuart England* (Liverpool, 1978).
130. See Paul Slack, 'Books of Orders: the Making of English Social Policy, 1577–1631', *Transactions of the Royal Historical Society*, 5th series, 30 (1980), 1–22; R.B. Outhwaite, *Dearth, Public Policy and Social Disturbance, 1550–1800* (Economic History Society, 1991).
131. Risdon, *Survey of Devon*, 328.
132. For later surviving surveys for Devon see Todd Gray (ed.), *Harvest Failure in Cornwall and Devon: The Book of Orders and the Corn Surveys of 1623 and 1630–1* (Camborne, 1992), 1–46; NDRO, B1/46/374.
133. HMC, Salisbury, XX (1968), 175.
134. Gray, *Harvest Failure*, xxxiv–xxxv; HMC, *Salisbury*, XX (1968), 284–5.
135. Drownings appear throughout the parish register and in the town records: Chanter and Wainwright, *Reprint*, I, 134.
136. Youings, 'Tudor Barnstaple', 10.
137. NDRO, Barnstaple parish register, burials. For plague in Devon see Paul Slack, *The Impact of Plague in Tudor and Stuart Devon* (Oxford, 1990 edn), 83–99.
138. NDRO, Barnstaple parish register, burials 1589.

EDITORIAL CONVENTIONS

Both copies of the Chronicle have been edited with the two combined into one account; the Hanmer copy has been printed in italic with the relevant passage placed immediately before its counterpart in Palmer's copy. All editorial conventions have been determined by the loss of the original chronicle and the subsequent uncertainties over whether these two surviving texts paraphrased the original. Consequently, letters or words which were crossed through or inserted by the copyists are included because some can be appreciated as significant (such as the substitution of the name Adam for Philip in the first line of Hanmer's copy) and any potential remaining ones could have an importance as yet unrecognized. For similar reasons original underlining, capitalization, spelling and punctuation have been retained. Modern spellings of current place-names are normally given only in the first occurrence. The numbering of some entries which appears in Palmer's copy has been retained. Archaic or uncertain words have been defined normally within a footnote or occasionally within square brackets in the text where it has been thought easier for the reader to understand. 'Ye' has been translated as 'the'. The original marginal notes which appear in Palmer's copy appear as such in this edition and any differences with the versions printed by the Lysons brothers and the *North Devon Magazine* are indicated in footnotes. Finally, this edition of Palmer's copy corrects some minor errors of transcription made by Chanter.

THE CHRONICLE

THE CHRONICLE

An extract of some particulars of of [sic] *Mr* ['Phillip Wioyts' crossed through, 'Adam Wyats' inserted] *townclarkes booke (being a journall) of things observeable in and about Barstaple, from An. Dom. 1586 unto An. 1611.*[1]

Extracts from an old Manuscript in the Possession of William Palmer of Barnstaple Clerk wrote by Philip Wyot Townclerke of Barnestaple beginning at the year 1586 to 1608.[2]

Fol. 1. 1586. A Book of matters carried on about the town of Barnstaple, and in various other places in Devon, subsequently to Easter, 1586, set down in English as follows[3]

1['6' corrected]*586. By the infection of the prisoners that were arraigned* [at] *the assises at Exeter before Easter, last, wch were sick of the*

1. 'Found at Poundisford Park believed to have been copied by Revd Jonathan Hanmer an ejected Minister of Bishops Tawton Devon in the Reign of Charles II' written in a letter hand.
2. On the inside cover is written
   'JR Chanter Fort Hill/Mons. Roch, Barnstaple this book was presented to me by Mrs Yeo a representative of Mr Roch relict of the above Mr Roch. He died in Jan. 7 1807. She died 27 Sep 1810 (Mr Roch *aged* 78) (Mrs Roch *aged* 84). John Roberts
   NB Who ever borrows these scraps of chronology of this town & vicinity of Barnestaple having perused them are desired not to lend them to any person but at the end of 14 days return them to Mr Roberts Boutportstreet as Mr R sets a value on them./Barnstaple.'
   On the inside page are listed 'fixed prices' of food items with a newspaper cutting of the same items which related to a Proclamation of 1315. Also on this page is
   'J.F. Chanter MA, FSA/Rector of Parracombe 1886–1916/Canon & Prebendary Exon 1920'
   On the first page is written
   'It[em blank]
   B. I find Philip Wyot stild Townclerk in 1558 [in later hand. NB Father of the Diarist]
   [in later hand written in blue ink. He appears afterwards in 1653 to have been Deputy Recorder & on April 12 1656 was dismissed for imbicility of mind & body & age. See Gribble pp. 297–297 [sic].
   This note of J.R.C.'s is answer. Philip Wyot dep. Recorder was an altogether diff. person see my Wyot pr disc. J.F.C.]'
   Attached to the inside back cover is a sheet of paper on which is written misc. notes relating to the mill at Barnstaple and Barnstaple Priory. The writing appears to be seventeenth century.
3. This was written in Latin: *Liber de Rebus gestis circa villa de Barnestap. … in com. Devn et in quibusdam aliis locis post fera Pasche Anno Dm. 1586, prout anglicis verbis sequuntur.*

gaoll sicknes,[4] *many men of worship and other that were ther at that time shortly after dyed thereof, viz. one of the justices of the assises called Mr* ['Bron' crossed through] *Baron Flowerdewe,*[5] *sir Arthur Basset knight,*[6] *sir John Chichester*[7] *and sir Barn*['e' inserted]*ard Drake knights, and Mr Walrond,*[8] *Mr Cary of Clavelly* [Clovelly],[9] *Mr Cary* [Carew] *of Hackome* [Haccombe], *Mr Fortescue, Mr Thomas Risedon*[10] *Justices of peace and diverse others of this shire of Devon. &c.*

—By the Infection of the Prisoners that were ['trying tried at' crossed through] arraynd the Assizes at Exeter before Easter las, among others died of the Gaoll sickness—died to wit [marginal note] Sir John Chechester Kt.

one of the Justices of Assize (viz) Mr. Flowerdewe, Sir Barnard Drak, Mr. Welrond Mr. Cary of Clavelly, Mr. Cary of Hackome Mr. Fortescue Mr. Rysdon Justices of peace

—Sir Arthur Basset died at Omberley [Umberleigh] and was buryed at Adryngton [Atherington].[11]

—Easter day dyed at Tawstock Lady Fitzwarren Mother to the Earl of Bath[12] [marginal note]

he was Lord Lieutanant of the county of Devon

4. A type of typhoid-fever. The 38 prisoners were Portugeuse men captured by Sir Bernard Drake in a raid on Newfoundland. It was claimed that they were 'cast into a deep pit and stinking dungeon [Rougemont Castle]': David B. Quinn (ed.), *New American World: A Documentary History of North America to 1612* (1979), IV, 48–9.
5. Edward Flowerdew was made treasurer of the Inner Temple in 1579 and third baron of the Exchequer in 1584: *The Concise Dictionary of National Biography* (Oxford, 1992), 1034.
6. Arthur Basset of Umberleigh was buried 2 April 1586 at Atherington: J.L. Vivian, *The Visitations of the Heralds to the County of Devon* (1895), I, 47.
7. He was Sheriff of Devon in 1585 and died 31 March 1586: Vivian, *Visitations*, I, 174.
8. Humphrey Walrond of Bradfield was buried at Uffculme on 7 April 1586: Vivian, *Visitations*, II, 768.
9. Robert Cary died 1 April 1586: Vivian, *Visitations*, I, 157.
10. Thomas Risdon of Parkham was double reader of the Inner Temple. He died on 2 April 1586: Vivian, *Visitations*, II, 649.
11. Sir Arthur Basset was born *c.*1528 and was buried on 2 April. There is a monument to him and his wife Eleanor in the parish church of Atherington with the inscription

    He that is 3 in 1 & 1 in 3
    it made us 2 then 1, this one were we
    One love, one life we lived—1 Year 1 Death
    Rocked us asleep by borrowing but 1 breath
    Grave the bed that holds us both—the Stone
    hides us covert—the bed is one
    1 Heaven contains our Souls—1 trump 1 day
    raise our bodies from this bed of clay
    Death which useth over to disever
    once united us for ever.

    : Richard Polwhele, *The History of Devonshire* (1977 edn), III, 407.
12. Frances, Lady Fitzwarren, was the daughter of Sir Thomas Kitson. Her memorial at Tawstock church, which noted 'she patiently departed this life in the true faith on Easter Day 1586', has the epitaph:

    Let spite and malice speake the truth what was this worthy wife,
    Who would some evil saie, yet cannot for their life.
    She many noted was to helpe and to doe hurte to none,
    Whom taken from the earth, her death both rich and poor do morn,
    Of honour vertue and renown, none could more plenty have.

—16 Ap: Year aforesd Sir Richard Greynvylle sailed ['out of Barnestaple' crossed through] over the Barr with his flee Boat & friget.[13] [marginal note] [marginal note a]
2—Corne is very deare. Wheate sold for viiis Rye for vis, Barley viiii p[er] bshel.[16]
3—The Wednesday before Whitsonday this year died Mrs. Elizabeth Chechester, late wife of Mr. Philipp Chechester at Taunton [Bishops Tawton],[17] and was buryed at Braunton, by her sayd husband.[18] [marginal note b]
—A ship of Sir Wm. Courtenay, who went to sea by force of letters of reprysals, and about May day took a French ship of 60 Tonnes laden with oyles, and in her dyvs. [divers] barrells of Coucheneall[21] besides xxiiii bagge of Ryalls[22] of plate & money cont[aining] in ev'y bagge iiii or 50 Ryalls, and arryved at Salcombe.[23]
4—George Pine chosen Mayor for the year ensuing.

but for want of suffict. water on the barr being neare upon neape,[14] he left his ship

[a] this Sir Richard Greynville pretended his goinge to Wyngandecora, where he was last year.[15]

[b] About this time commandemt given that the Beacons sh[oul]d be reedified[19] & diligently watched day and night, and that post horses shd be p[ro]vided in evy town, and that evy pson shd p[ro]vide in rediness his armour.[20]

On Michaelmas eve this year the weather being very fowle, ther arose such a tempest of winde, that it made the water at the kay so arise, that they that were upon the kay and saw it, could not see['th' crossed through] *the marsh: it went upward and ripped diverse houses between Mr Wourths lane and the fish-shambles; and so in that breadth in it went east through the towne blowing downe much covering of houses: it was about 4 of the clock in the afternoone.*

13. Fly boat: a fast-sailing vessel used for rapid transport of goods, in voyages of exploration and for warlike purposes. Frigate: a light and swift vessel originally used for rowing, a larger vessel generally used by merchantmen or a larger vessel used for war.
14. The neap tide, shortly after the first and third quarters of the moon when the high-water level is at its lowest.
15. Grenville had sailed from Plymouth in April 1585 for the West Indies and along the Atlantic seaboard to 'Wyngandecora', what is now North Carolina. In contrast, the voyage in 1587 was not for exploration but privateering. See David Quinn, *New American World*, III, 265–314.
16. The Lysons brothers noted that the Chronicle stated barley was priced at five shillings and four pence: Daniel & Samuel Lysons, *Magna Britannia; being a Concise Topographical Account of the Several Counties of Great Britain: Volume the sixth containing Devonshire* (1822), 31.
17. 'Tawton': *North Devon Magazine* copy, 153
18. Elizabeth Chichester was buried on 21 May 1586: NDRO, Braunton parish register.
19. Reedify: to rebuild.
20. Beacons remained an issue: *CSPD 1580–1591*, 635; Six shillings and eight pence were paid to Scampe, the cutler, for 'scouring and keeping clean the harness and armour' belonging to the corporation: Chanter and Wainwright, *Barnstaple Records*, 107.
21. Cochineal: the scarlet dye-stuff made from dried insects.
22. Rials: an English coin originally valued at ten shillings and also a French coin; reals, a Spanish coin or plate.
23. Courtenay's choice of Salcombe was probably due to his having the nearby residence of Ilton Castle.

5—Very high flood in September wind at W.
7—October 1586 Thomas Hinson[24] and Lewes ['Danse' crossed through] Darke[25] gentlemen were ['chosen' crossed through] elected and chosen for the burgesses of this town of Barn. for the Parliament next comyng.[26]
—On St. Luke's day [18 October] this yere there was a trental[27] of sermons at Pylton [Pilton], so that divers as well men as women rode and went thither, they called it an exercise or holy faste and there some offerd as they did when they went on pilgrimage.
—And the like was kept at Sherwill to the admiracon of all P[ro]testants.[28]
—In december this year Sir Richard Greynfild came home bringing a prise [prize] with him laden with sugar ginger & hyds.
8—7 Feb. 1586 [1587] My Lord of Bath & Mr. H Ackland Justices sat here at this towne for the direction of corne to be brought to this market and for the maintenance of the poor within their own p[ari]shes. and none to go abroad, so that somme of evy. p[ari]sh. appointed to view barnes and mows[29] and to take a note what store of corn their was and what people were in such houses as had corne to spare, and allowing evy pson a peck a weke to certify the overplus to the said Justices, but what[30] good this order will do the comon .... buyers of corne many stand in doubt, beause now corne being deare, viz., wheate at viiis the bushel, they feare this order may make it dearer as it did last yere.[31]

24. Hinson was part of the household of the Earl of Bath and was buried at Tawstock parish church in 1614. He continued to represent Barnstaple in Parliament in 1589, 1597 and 1604. Dart was the son of a Barnstaple merchant and former mayor as well as member of Parliament. He later represented Tregony and died in Cornwall in 1632: Daphne Drake, 'Members of Parliament for Barnstaple, 1492–1688', *Transactions of the Devonshire Association* LXXII (1940), 255–6.
25. Lewis Darte, of Barnstaple and Pentewan in Cornwall, was baptized 19 May 1562, married Elizabeth Roscarrock and died in 1632: Haslam, *House of Commons*, II, 20.
26. The sessions dates were 29 October to 2 December 1586 and 15 February to 23 March 1587.
27. Trentals: a set of thirty.
28. The Lysons' copy repeated the two sentences exactly except for 'they went in pilgrimage': Lysons, *Magna Britannia*, 33.
29. Mow: a stack of hay, corn, beans, peas, etc. or a heap of grain or hay in a barn. Mowhay: a loft or chamber for storing grain in Devon and Cornwall.
30. The Lysons brothers noted that the copy of the Chronicle recorded 'what good this order will do many doubt, because new corn being dear, they fear this order may make it dearer, as it did last year': Lysons, *Magna Britannia*, 31.
31. The Book of Orders was first issued that year: Paul Slack, 'Books of Orders: the Making of English Social Policy, 1577–1631', *Transactions of the Royal Historical Society*, Fifth series, 30 (1980), 3. In 1587 the Braunton churchwardens paid six pence for the constables expenses in travelling to Barnstaple and another eight pence for viewing the corn: NDRO, 1677A/PW1A.

9—24 Feb. A general muster of [sic] here at Barn. before my Lord of Bath, Sr Richard Greynfild, Mr. Hugh Acland, and Mr. George Wyot Justices of all the able men with a shew of their arms & furniture[32] of the hundred of Braunton[33] Shyrwill [Shirwell] and Fremyngton [Fremington].
—And on Wednesday following the inhabitants of this town & parish mustred before the sd Justices in the Church with a shewe of their arms and ['furniture' crossed through] artillery.
10—The xith of March Lorde Fitzwarren, eldest son and heire of Lord Bathe, died at Tawstock suddenly, but xvi months old.[34]

1587.

—at Lent Assize only one Judge, viz., Mr. Baron Gent.
11—The dearthe of corne yet remains, wheate at viiis & yet this countrye is dailey further charged with ammunition and harness, expecting & p[ro]viding for invasions and warrs which maketh the common sort fall into poverty for want of trade, so that div[er]s fall to robbynge & stealinge, the like hath never been seen.[35]

{April 2nd Corn dear—wheat 8s, rye 6s, barley 5s 4d per bushel}

About May.

—little or no raine hath fallen for vi or viii weeks whereby more Dearthe and Scarcity is to be lookt for.[36]
12—May cccc bushels of rye arrived—not above lxxx b[ushe]ls sold—wheate rose next market day to ixs—girts[37] vis viii—barley vis viii.
—June ccccccc bls of rye at the p[ro]curement of some of this town were brought here whereby wheat fell from xs a bushel to viiis vid—which rye was sold for vis a bushel.
13—at Assizes at Exeter, before Lord Anderson[38] & Baron Gente[39] one

32. Furniture: armour, accoutrements, weapons, etc.
33. The Braunton churchwarden accounts shows a payment of 7s 8d for the mustering at Barnstaple. There was also training at Raleigh in the parish of Pilton: NDRO, 1677A/PW1A.
34. He was buried on the 12th of March, 1587: NDRO, Tawstock parish register.
35. On 19 February 1587/8 there was 'a base child which was born in the street': NDRO, Barnstaple parish register.
36. The Lysons brothers noted that in the copy they examined it was written 'whereby more dearth and scarcity was to be looked for': Lysons, *Magna Britannia*, 31.
37. Girts: coarsely ground oats.
38. In 1582 Edmund Anderson was knighted and made lord chief justice of common pleas. At the time of this visit to Barnstaple he already taken part in the trials of Babbington and Mary Queen of Scots and later part of those of the earl of Essex and Sir Walter Raleigh: *DNB*, III, 50.
39. Sir Thomas Gent was a barrister of the Middle Temple, baron of the Exchequer in 1586 and member of the High Commission court: *DNB*, 1120.

Menarde of Exon, had his ears cut of his nostrils slutte and burnt in the face with an hot iyron wth the l[ette]re S[40]
—August Wheat sold for ivs, rye for iis viii, barley iis iiid, by reason of the plenty of new corne.[41]
14[42]—Lord Bath & the Countess his wyfe dyned at the new Mr. Maiors—the women this yeare were not bidden wherefore there was much chatteringe among them.[43]

—October a pcept from Ld Bath to the maior to warne those sette to light horses[44] to appear at Torrington with ryders and necessaries &c before Mr. ['Justice' crossed through] Lewes Pollard.[45]
15—Mr. Hugh Fortescue and Mr. Robert Dillon[46] kept their Christmas here belike for saving of Charges &c.
—Wheate sold for iiis vid, barley iid [sic] ii, oats xiiid[47]
—xxvi february went to see the workinge of the silver mynes at Combm'ten [Combe Martin].[48]
—this day[49] Ld Baths son was Xtned [christened] called Roberte[50] godfa[the]r Sr Richd Greynfylde for Ld Chancellor, Sir Williem

40. This was noted as 'June 14th', the prisoner is referred to as 'Menardo' and the letter was 'F': *North Devon Magazine* copy, 154.
41. 'by reason of the plenty of new corn'. Lysons noted that wheat was priced at ten shillings: Lysons, *Magna Britannia*, 31.
42. 'June 14th': *North Devon Magazine* copy, 154.
43. That year the town paid £3 12s 8d for dinner 'for my Lord of Bath, the Countess his wife, Sir Thomas Dennys, Mr Cary and divers other gentlemen with their trains being in town this 23 of May': NDRO, B1/3972/130.
44. Light cavalry.
45. The Earl of Bath reported from Exeter on 7 December to the Privy Council on the county's militia: *CSPD 1581–1590*, 443. On 21 December Sir Walter Raleigh wrote to Lord Burghley regarding the costs: *CSPD 1581–1590*, 445. See also pages 469, 547.
46. Robert Dillon lived at 'Hart'[?land]. He was baptized on 27 March 1582: Vivian, *Visitations*, I, 285.
47. 'August 15th': *North Devon Magazine* copy, 154; The copy which the Lysons brothers examined recorded that at Christmas 1587 the price of wheat had fallen to 2s 8d, barley 2s 2d and oats 1s 6d: Lysons, *Magna Britannia*, 32.
48. The mines at Combe Martyn were working during the reign of Edward I but had ceased any activity for some time. They were reopened in this year by Adrian Gilbert and one Mr Bulmer, a mining expert. The mine was active until 1593 and then sporadically until 1875. Two cups were made and presented to the Lord Mayor of London and to the Earl of Bath. On the latter it was inscribed

In Martyn's Combe long lay I hydd,
Obscured, deprest with grossest soyle,
Debased much with mixed lead,
Till Bulmer came; whose skill and toyle
Refined mee so pure and cleene,
As rycher no where els is seene.

And addinge yet a darfer grace,
By fashion he did inable
Mee worthy for to take a place,
To serve at any Prince's table,
Combe Martyne gave the use alone,
Bulmer, the fyning and fashion.

The London cup was melted down in 1643: Hoskins, *Devon*, 136–8.
49. 'Oct. 15th': *North Devon Magazine* copy, 154.
50. They were all godparents. The baby was baptized on the 3rd of March 1588 and buried on the 27th of May: NDRO, Tawstock parish register.

Mown[51] for the E. of Essex,[52] Lady Denys for the old Countess of Bedford.

1588.

17—Fine weather in March.
—Wheat sold for iis viii barley xxd, rye xxii[53] ots xid ['at 12 gallons' crossed through][54]
18—5 ships[55] went over the bar to join Sr F[rancis] D[rake] at plymo.[56]
—200 trayned souldiers of Braunton and Fremington H[undre]ds. viewed in the Castle Green by Mr. H. Fortescue their Capt.
19—Mr. Hugh Fortescue removed his household again to Weare [Giffard].[57]
—Wheate sold for iis ivd, rye xxd, ots xi, barley xvi.
22—much afraid of a Spanish Invasion.[58]
—3 August. Sr Ed. Anderson Ch. Justice of com' place and Mr. Baron Gente dyned with Mr. Maior, supped with Mr. Lewis Darke—sunday dyned at Leigh with Mr. G. Wyot, lodged at Ackland [Acland Barton],[59] from thence went to Clavelly & staid with Mr. Carye, sherif of Devon in their way to Ireland.[60]

51. Sir William Mohun of Hall near Fowey and later of Boconnoc in Cornwall: A.L. Rowse, *Tudor Cornwall* (1957), 331.
52. Robert Devereux was executed three years later on 25 February 1601.
53. 'barley 1s 8d rye 1s 10d': *North Devon Magazine* copy, 154.
54. The copy the Lysons brothers examined observed wheat was priced at 2s 8d, barley 1s 8d, rye 1s 10d and oats 11d: Lysons, *Magna Britannia*, 32.
55. 'Six ships': *North Devon Magazine* copy, 154.
56. This reference to the five ships has long been in dispute. It has been shown that these vessels were part of a squadron of ships from the Torridge being prepared by Sir Richard Grenville for North Carolina: A.L. Rowse, *Sir Richard Grenville of the Revenge* (1940), 255–66; Joyce Youings, 'North Devon at Sea', *The Official Souvenir Programme of the Celebrations in North Devon to mark the 400th Anniversary of the Spanish Armada* (North Devon Journal, 1988), 21. The fleet at Plymouth comprised some 197 ships: Colin Martin & Geoffrey Parker, *The Spanish Armada* (1988). On 8 April the mayors of Barnstaple and Great Torrington wrote to the Privy Council that they were unable to send ships to Drake: *CSPD 1581–1590*, 474. On the first of the month the Privy Council had requested two ships and a pinnace to be supplied by the two towns: *Acts of the Privy Council, 1588*, 9. See also pages 147–8, 201, 272; The Lysons brothers noted that 'the port of Barnstaple fitted out three ships for the fleet which defeated the Spanish Armada in 1588': Lysons, *Magna Britannia*, 34.
57. Weare Giffard Hall was the home of the Fortescues from 1454 and later became the second residence of the family: Cherry & Pevsner, *Devon*, 891–2.
58. There were several months of apprehension. Although the Armada sailed by Plymouth on 31 July it continued on to the North Sea by 7 August and the remants of the fleet were off the Irish coast two months later. The only Spanish ship to come ashore in Devon, besides prizes such as the *Nuestra Senora del Rosario*, was the wreck of the *San Pedro Mayor* at Hope Cove on the south coast: Paula Martin, *Spanish Armada Prisoners* (Exeter, 1988), 48–50; Barnstaple's fears of an invasion are somewhat legitimized by a later report that the Spanish attempted to ascertain navigational information regarding the rivers Taw and Torridge: *CSPD 1595–1597*, 213.
59. The original home of the Acland family, located in Landkey parish. Among the remaining features is a doorway with the date 1591: Bridget Cherry & Nikolaus Pevsner, *Devon* (1989), 125.
60. The Irish campaign figures greatly in the borough's records for this year: Chanter and Wainwright, *Reprint*, 107; the Braunton churchwardens gave £3 6s 8d to the justices when 'the soldiers were going into Ireland': NDRO, 1677A/PW1A.

25—The fair this year was kept Monday the ix September because there sh[oul]d be no buying & selling Sunday.[61]
—xvii Octr. Mr. Thomas Leigh,[62] gent. an utter barrister[63] was sworne deputy recorder to my Lord of Bath.
27—Thomas Hinson, Esquyer, and John Dodderidge,[64] chosen ['members' crossed through] burgesses for this town to be at parliament.[65]
—continual rayne.
—wheat rose to iiiis vd
29—victuals & grayne very plenty, best beef for 1d pr pound, wheat iiis, rye & barley xviiid pr b[ushe]l.[66]

An. 1588 upon the Fryday before Passion sunday ther were heer in the market about 110 fat beeves[67] *and above, the like number had not been seen before in the* ['A' crossed through] *market the like day.*

—110 fat oxen in the Market one day the like never seen before on Friday before Easter.[68]

1589.

Order from Ld Bath to the Con[sta]bles of Braunton hundred to p[ro]vide Vc [500] bushels of wheate, & so much butter & cheese conveniently to be got in h[undred] of Braunton to be sent after Sr F. Drake's fleet.
32—Mr. Henery Chechester of Arlington died at Exeter in July of a

61. The fair was normally held on 8 September, the feast of the Nativity of the Virgin Mary, except when that date fell on a Sunday: Chanter & Wainwright, *Reprint*, I, 58–9.
62. Thomas Leigh was presumably of Northam: Vivian, *Visitations*, II, 528.
63. For discussion of the legal profession see Wilfred Prest, 'Lawyers', in Wilfred Prest (ed.), *The Professions in Early Modern England* (1987), 64–89.
64. Dodderidge was paid £3 6s 8d for his expenses: Wainwright, *Reprint*, II, 103. Dodderidge was born in about 1555, the son of a merchant of South Molton and Barnstaple. Dodderidge was a barrister of the Middle Temple, Serjeant-at-law in 1604, Solicitor General from 1604 to 1607 and Judge of the Queen's Bench from 1612 to 1628. He was also mayor of Barnstaple in 1579 and was one of the counsel to the town. He married Joan Jerman and Dorothy Hancock (both of Exeter) and Anne Culme. He died on 13 September 1628: Drake, 'Members', 256; Haslam, *House of Commons*, I, 42.
65. The date of the summons was 18 September 1588 for 12 November and was prorogued 14 October. The sessions dates were 4 February to 29 March 1589.
66. 'October Wheat 3s Rye and Barley 1s 6d Beef 1d per lb': *North Devon Journal* copy, 154.
67. Plural of beef.
68. The copy which the Lysons brothers examined had this information and the previous entry relating to grain prices: Lysons, *Magna Britannia*, 32.

squinzie[69] in his throat, he was a notable wise and discreet gentleman and did appease many controversies among his neighbrs and his death greatly lamented.
—North peere (called Maiden Arches), of the great [Long] bridge built on wood taken down and rebuilt in three weeks on an arch cost xxvi pounds.[70]
33—Unicorn, a reprisal Ship of this Town sent in a price [prize].
—John Norrys[71] with his bark returned having been a reprising.[72]
34—Vicar is excommunicated.[73]
—Mr. Robert Appley the elder by his will gave great charity to this towne.[74]
35. About this time (March) great wain[75] of rain—none in vi weeks.

1590.

36—dyed Sir John Clarys Clarke vicar of Barnestaple.[76]
—22 Maye. Edward Chechester of Arlington was stabbd with a dagger by one Gamon a captn. of a ship & was killed.[77]
—Wheat vis. viiid. Vituals dearer.
—A pickard[78] loden with barley malt from the Foreste,[79] arrived to sell for iiis the b[ushe]l.
—July 8 ships saild over our bar for Rochelle.[80]
—Masers & cherries very plenty.[81]
—divers have cut Corn before St. James Day [25 July]
—Harvest ended in many places before midst of August.[82]

---

69. Squinancy, squinsy or quinsy: a disease of the throat or suppurative tonsillitis.
70. This was recorded by a stone inscription with 'R[obert]P[rowse]M[ayor] 1589 H[enry]D[owne] B[ridge]W[warden]: Gribble, *Barnstaple*, 565.
71. He was buried in Barnstaple on 31 December 1610: NDRO, Barnstaple parish register.
72. In the spring of 1588 Norris petitioned the Privy Council for letters of marque: *Acts of the Privy Council, 1587–1588*, 427.
73. He died shortly afterwards.
74. Robert Appley gave the tenement of Congerham in Newport: Gribble, *Memorials*, 108.
75. Wane: a want or shortage.
76. He was buried on 30 April 1590: NDRO, Barnstaple parish register. The following entry was that of the burial of his servant, Phillip Demonde, on 3 May.
77. Edward Chichester was buried at Pilton on 24 May. The parish register also recorded that he was wounded on 22 May: NDRO, Barnstaple parish register.
78. Picard: a large sailing boat or barge used for coastal or river traffic.
79. Most likely from the Severn Valley.
80. The port of La Rochelle was favoured for the purchase of salt.
81. Mazards: the dark cherry, remain a favourite in North Devon.
82. The copy the Lysons brothers examined had the same corn prices and notes on the harvest: Lysons, *Magna Britannia*, 32.

37—On account of plague of pestilence[83] assizes held at Honyton [Honiton] before C. Justice Anderson & Gente—Gente went to Exeter opend Comn at Castle and adjourn to Honyton—xvii prisoners executed the most part for murder.
—plague much at Totness [Totnes].[84]
39—the prudence a ship of 100 tons belonging to Mr. Dodderidge of this town with fourscore men saild over the bar on a reprisal voyage.

An. 1590. This year one Ferres a Pursevaunt[85] *gave out much money upon great gaine, that he with a Pilot and one more with him would go in a whirrey-boat*[86] *by water from Thames to Bristow* [Bristol]*: so on midsomer day he departed out of Thames and the first day of August following he arrived at Ilfardecombe* [Ilfracombe] *and the same day the weather being fair and calme he departed ther hence towards Bristow.*

—Michaelmas Sessions held at Great Torrington, the plague being much[87] at Exeter.[88]

The saturday being St Stevens day [26 December] *this year, ther came in over the bar of Barum and arrived at Appledor* [Appledore 'of' crossed through, 'a' inserted] *ship of this towne called the Prudence of 100 tonnes and belonging to Mr Dodderidge of this towne and others (she* ['set' crossed through] *sayled* ['over' inserted] *the bar of Barnestaple in a reprisall voiage on St Mathewes day* [21 September] *this year having in her 80 men or above) and brought in a prize*[89] *with her being a Portugall ship of about 80 tonns, wch had been at* ['Castlle' crossed through] *Castellmayne upon the coast of Gynney, having in her 4 chests of gold to the value of 16,000 pounds, and diverse chains of gold with Civet,*[90] *Ambergreece*[91] *and other things of great price, with much*

83. It was probably merely coincidence that the Barnstaple parish burials for this year include those of five older people. They were 'the old Johan Chinge', 'the old Johan Hayne', 'the old mother Yeane widow', 'Thomas Norris aged 91' and 'the old mother Bowden': NDRO, Barnstaple parish register, burials 1589.
84. In 1590–91 there were 285 burials at Totnes. The yearly average was 52.7: Slack, *Impact of Plague*, 90.
85. Pursuivant: a junior heraldic officer.
86. Wherry, a light rowing boat or a barge.
87. 'plague raging at Exeter': *North Devon Magazine* copy, 155.
88. In St Mary Major parish alone there were 142 burials in 1590–91 when the average was 31.5: Slack, *Impact of Plague*, 90.
89. This was the *Holy Spirit* of Lisbon: Grant, *Atlantic Adventurer*, 8.
90. Civet: a perfume with a strong musk-like smell.
91. Ambergris: a fragrant waxy substance derived from the spermaceti whale and used in the production of perfume.

graynes, Ele['peh' crossed through]*phant tooth &c. such a value as the like price hath not before this time been brought into this port. This ship was brought up unto the kay of Barum aforesaid the third day next following. the said chests of gold did weigh about* ['320' crossed through] *320 pound weight of gold, besides many chaines of gold wherof the company made pillage.*[92]

40—arrived the prudence with a price taken on the coast of Guinney [Guinea] having in her iiii chest of gold to the value of xvi thousand pounds & divers chaynes of gold with civet and other things of great value such a price as this was never brought into this port.
—price [prize] about Cxxx ton brought to key head at Barn: chests & baskets of gold weighed cccxx pound.

Monday the 16th of march this year the assises were kept at this town (exeter being infected with the plague) by Judge Anderson alone: the places for him to sit in were made upon the kay, the one ag[ains]*t the kayhall* [quay hall], *and the other by the north end of Mr Collyberes house and were both covered with rude:*[93] *Mr Roger Beaple was now maior: Mr Medford parson of of* [sic] *Combmerten preached on tewesday. 16th of march, before the judge, 18 were condemned the wenesday and executed at the Castle the saturday following in the afternoone at wherof Mrs Paige was one.*

B—March great p[ro]vision making for holding the assizes in this towne.
41—the places for the judges to sit it, one against the keyhall [Quay Hall] & the other by the north end of Mr. Collibear's house both coverd with rude.
42—There came hither but 1 judge Ld. Anderson he came to town the Monday in the afternoon to the keyhall place there where he sat all the assizes, read the commission, charged the grand jury & adjourned.

---

92. 'The Prudence brought hither a prize worth 10,000 l': *North Devon Magazine* copy, 155.
93. Reed.

—the tuesday, the Judge Ld. Bath & other Gent, dind with Mr. Mayor.[94]
—Martyne the gaoler kept some of his prisonrs in house late Bailiffs in this towne, and others in Castle Green under tylts[95] with sayles.
—Judge lodged at Mr. Doddridges.
—Sherif at Mawdlene [priory of St Mary Magdalene].[96]
—Serjt. Drue at Gilb. Harriss.
—Serjt. Glandyl at Rog. Cades.
—Serjt. Harrys at Mr. W. Collibears.
—Mr. Heale at Mr. Welshes house.
Rest of the lawyers well accommodated elsewhere.
—Tuesday sat on nisi prius.[97]
—Wednesday by 5 o clock the judg tried ii or iii causes of nisi prius & then upon the gaol, continued the Wednesday & gave judgement upon those who were to be executed.
—Friday & Saturday sat on nisi prius & ended.
—The gibbet was sat up on the Castle Green and xviii prisoners hangd, whereof iiii of plymouth for a murder.[98]

1591.

44—March vituals about [in pencil. this] time very dear.
—about witsontide xix nobles[99] was given for a heifer that had new calf.[100]
—Plague of pestilence at Southmolton & Torrington.[101]
—the last of June the wief of Ambrose Wilkey of Pilton Tanner leapt

94. This year a buck was sent from Tawstock and the vension was baked in the town: NDRO, B1/3972/137.
95. Tilts: an awning or covering, a tent.
96. The Lysons' copy repeated this exactly except for 'prisoners in the house', 'on the Castle green': Lysons, *Magna Britannia*, 34.
97. Nisi prius: a writ directed to a sheriff commanding him to provide a jury at Westminster on a specified day unless the assize judges previously come to the county.
98. Eighteen skeletons were found in about 1864 buried 'thrown together in a heap' at the Castle. The Plymouth murder was the notorious case of Ulalia Page who was convicted of the murder of her husband: Chanter, *Sketches*, 37, 10–13; The Lysons copy noted 17 prisoners were hanged: Lysons, *Magna Britannia*, 34.
99. Noble: gold coin first minted by Edward III.
100. 'Jan. 24th': *North Devon Magazine* copy, 155.
101. In 1592–3 sixteen shillings were paid at Barnstaple 'towards the relief of the inhabitants of the town of Great Torrington': Chanter and Wainwright, *Reprint*, II, 131.

over Barnestaple Bridge, was seen by William Davy who swam to her the tide being half out & savd her & deliverd her to her husband.
—pease & beans sell in their cods[102] for xiid a bushel.[103]
—This somer Assizes held at South Teavistocke [marginal notes], the Judges were Ld Anderson & Mr. Gente they held it in Abbey Green under a Tylt—also the Quarter Sessions held there—xiii pris[one]rs executed at the Assizes. Teavistock Tavistock
46—The prudence of Barne. sent home 2 prices [prizes].
—Watchmen continually to prevent suspected folks of the plague from coming into town.[104]
—Mr. Mayor all this yeare at every courte holden at the Guildhall kept a dynner for the aldermen & others that there resorte of the messes not being bound thereto but of his own liberalitie.
—Mr. Maior hath taken great pains and travayle to pserve this towne from infection of the plague.[105]
48—Great store of sider this yere wch maketh cask deare a hoxede [hogshead] is sold for iiis & a pipe for vis.
—12th Octr a bark of this town wch had been a reprising called the White Hart put into Ilfordcombe [Ilfracombe] brought home som elifants' teth.[106]

An. 1591. sir Rich: Greynfield in the Revenge one of the queens ships about the beginning of Sept. encountred with the whole Spanish fleet being 70 saile wherof they slew many men but were faine to yield at last upon composition for their lives and libertyes. This fight began in the afternoon, continued all the next night and until ten of the clock the next day.

—same day report came that her Majestys ship at sea Sr Richard Greynfild Captaine was taken by the Spaniards after encountring the whole Spanish Fleet for 2 daies.

102. 'pods': *North Devon Magazine* copy, 155.
103. The copy which the Lysons brothers examined had the same note of the peas and beans as well as of the heifer: Lysons, *Magna Britannia*, 32.
104. 'Watchmen continually employed to prevent persons, suspected of having the plague, from entering the town': *North Devon Magazine* copy, 155; Thirteen watchmen were paid to exclude from the fair those from infected places: Chanter and Wainwright, *Reprint*, II, 131.
105. Thirteen watchmen were appointed to 'keep out from the fair those that came from places infected with the plague': Wainwright, *Reprints*, II, 131.
106. Ivory.

49—Corn is somewhat reasonable I bought wheat for iis viiid.[107]
—a pinnace called the *fortmouth* a reprisal ship of this harbour brought in a price [prize] laden with wynes.
—xxvth January the *prudence* brought in over this Bar a price worth x thousand pounds.
50—pclamation to make Kersies[108] xv yards in length and xvlb in weight[109]

1592.

55—In September October & November was the church thoroughly painted within & divers texts of scripture wroten on the pillars, and the Iuylds [aisles] began to be painted
—died my Father Philip Wyat at Braunton[110]
—the Knights of the Shire were chosen at Exeter Sir Thomas Dennys Kt.[111] and Mr. Seamor esquyer.
—xii february Mr. Geo. Chippinge[112] a gentleman of my Lord of Bath and Richard Leye[113] were appointed by common Counsell to be Burgesses for this parliamt & so returned by indenture to the Sherif.[114]

1593.

—iii subsidies and vi fifteenths granted by parliamt to be paid her Majty with iii yeares.
—the white Hart is taken.
—because of the long drieth this yere people from Hartland came to Rayleigh [Raleigh] & Brodeford [Bradiford] Mills with griests [corn].
—the Gifte a reprisal ship of this towne belonging to W. Morcomb of this towne & others carried a rich price into Ilfordcombe [Ilfracombe].

107. The copy which the Lysons examined also had the same price for wheat: Lysons, *Magna Britannia*, 32.
108. Kersies, a narrow cloth which had a coarse texture and light weight: Joyce Youings, *Tucker's Hall Exeter, The History of a Provincial City Company Through Five Centuries* (Exeter, 1968), 2.
109. For regulations in the making of Devon kersies see Youings, *Tucker's Hall*, 2–4, 37–9.
110. 'Phillip Wyott sen. gent.' was buried on 23 December 1592: NDRO, Braunton parish register.
111. Sir Thomas Dennys of Holcombe Rogus was born in 1559, married Anne, daughter of Sir William Paulet, and died in 1613. He was Sheriff of Devon in 1594: Haslam, *House of Commons*, II, 32.
112. George Chittinge was the son of Henry Chittinge of Wortham, Suffolk: Haslam, *House of Commons*, I, 603.
113. Ley was elected a freeman of Barnstaple in 1593: Drake, 'Members', 256–7.
114. The summons date was 4 January and the sessions were 19 February to 10 April 1593. There was a payment by the town of one shilling for indentures regarding the election: Wainwright, *Reprint*, II, 103.

—Sir John St. leger & others Justices of this North Division met about rating the subsidy.

An. 1593. ther is to be paid this year ['to' crossed through, 'by' inserted] *her majesty's subjects one whole subsidy and two Quindteins*[115] *out of hand: such an imposition as ther is not recorded was ever layd upon the subjects of this land by any Prince.*

—i subsidy & ii quindecims to be paid out of hand.
57—later end of September the river at Bradiford was frozen over.
—xii novr dyed Clemente Burton[116] was sometime servante and secretaire to the old Sr. John Chechester Kt.[117] and livd a Batchelor he was accounted a wise man & a good Scholar and would buy and have the most part of all new Books made whereby he had a great Librarie & was buryed in the Iuyld [aisle] at Pylton [Pilton].

1593.
—The Chayms [chimes] now going wch coste besides the bell that was had before xxvl—a great charge to small effect.
—Rain & violent winds every day in March, the shyppyng cod. not go to Newfondland or Rochelle or those at Rochelle come home.

1594.
—price of corn near at one price.
—['Wheat about vs. barley & rye iiis. ii the bushel, ots xviii' crossed through in pencil][118]
—['Wheat at viis vid' crossed through]
—15th Septr. died my bro[the]r Geo: Wyat at Leigh.[119]
—Mr. John Chechester of Westcott [Westacott] in Marwood had a servant maiden hangd herself at the buttery door.
—pclamation published forbydding the wearing of dagg[er]s or pistolles.

115. Quindecim: a tax or duty of one fifteenth part of each man's goods.
116. He was buried at Pilton on 13 November: NDRO, Barnstaple parish register.
117. The wall monument to Sir John Chichester is in St Mary's church, Pilton: Cherry & Pevsner, *Devon*, 629.
118. The copy which the Lysons brothers examined had these same prices: Lysons, *Magna Britannia*, 32.
119. He was buried on 17 September: NDRO, Barnstaple parish register.

—All the brewsters & tiplers[120] of ale within the H[undred] of Braunton & Sherwell [Shirwell] appd at Barn before Mr. Dyllon & Mr. Ackland justices & bound by recogn to keep good rule &c.
—in March John Darke of Pylton [Pilton] a frysemaker[121] began to erect & buyld a wind mill at the higher end of Pylton be east the priorie there upon the lands of Mr. Henry Rolle.
59—Francis Hawkins was hung in chains at Highbickington for the murder of a Cornishman a sailor.

1595.
—one Cesar brother[122] of Dr. [Julius] Cesar came from the Admiraltri with a commission to seale the beaze[123] and new made cloths.
60. Orders from the [Privy] Councill that on intelligence of 2 or 3 Spanish ships being sent into St. Georges Channel[124] the Maior was to provide a shipp of this harbour to rencounter with them—her Maj-[es]ty w[oul]d. bear one half of the charge and this country adjoyning to bear the other half,—the justices appointed John Barrett of this towne Captayn of a new made shipp of William Morcome for the service which Mr. Maior of this town & his brethren do well leke of.
—Mr. John Chechester eldest son of Mr. John Chechester of Hall came into this towne to dwell from his house at Westcott [Westacott]
—By reason of rayn and foul weather wheat is ixs a b[ushe]l.[125]
—xxx of August Ld. B[isho]pp came to town was met in Southgate Street by the Maior & Maisters in their scarlet gowns, a skolar made a speech, afterwards the Bp dind with Mr. Maior.[126]
—he confirmed div[er]s children at the Castle Green, on the 2d day such a Multitude came in from the country that he cod. scarce pass the

120. Tippler: a retailer of ale and other alcoholic beverages.
121. Frieze: coarse woollen cloth with a nap.
122. This was Sir Thomas Caesar, 1561–1610, brother of Sir Julius, judge of the Admiralty: *Dictionary of National Biography*, 434.
123. Bay, or baize: a fine and light wool cloth.
124. The Bristol Channel.
125. On 1 August 1595 the Justices at Exeter reported to the Privy Council that the price of corn was falling throughout the county except near Plymouth: DRO, DQS, OB 1, 122.
126. A banquet was given by the town for 'Mr Dean and his company being in the bishop's visitation': NDRO, B1/3972.

street, on a sudden he turned up Crockstreet[127] & went to his lodgings, & went out of towne almost forthence—the people lamented they had lost a fine harvest day.[128]
70—28 novr E. of Bath Mr. Pollard, Mr Carey Mr. Abbot justices sat at the Guildhall where they had calld all the con[sta]bles. of the Nth. Division to give notice to those that were sett to arms to be in readyness and that the billes shd. be chaungd into pykes, and the bows and arrowes into Muskitts and Calyvers.[129]

xith decr John Norrys a burges of this town brought a new charter to town which I red in Englysh[130] before the Maior & most part of the comon council.[131]

An. 1595. The monday being the 15th of december, Mr George Pyne maior, and Roger Cade and James Beaple Aldermen of Barum by vertue of the new Charter were sworn justices of the peace within the Borough of Barum, and the said Aldermen were sworn coroners for this year following.

—the 2 aldermen the Ist. coroners in town.
—Thomas Skynner a common counselman elected clerke of the market according to new charter & sworne, &c.
—Newfo[u]ndland fishery stoppd by order of High Admiral.
73—came to towne the Queens Takers to take up fat oxen for p[ro]vision at Plymouth and drew Tikets upon the high Sherif for payment.
—The constables of Braunton hundred had orders to levy five marks in money & xii flitchys of bacon[132] @ iiii a pound to be sent likewise to Plymouth.
—In March a Commandmant from the privy counsel was brought that this towne shd. sett forthe the prudence beinge about 100 tons burthen

127. Crock Street was the traditional market place for local potters: Alison Grant, 'Stopping up the Market Place: Crock Street and Barnstaple's Potters in the Seventeenth Century', 86–8, in Todd Gray (ed.), *Devon Documents* (Exeter, 1996).
128. Gervase Babington was nominated 22 March 1594, confirmed 11 March 1595 and was translated to Worcester 4 October 1597; The Lysons' copy repeated this passage exactly except for 'dined with the Mayor': Lysons, *Magna Britannia*, 34.
129. Caliver: a light kind of musket or harquebus.
130. 'John Norrys, a burgess, brought a new charter to the town, which was read in English': *North Devon Magazine* copy, 155.
131. Wyatt received thirty-eight shillings and eight pence for copying the charter 'and other work': Chanter and Wainwright, *Reprint*, II, 145.
132. Flitches: side of an animal, generally a hog, which was salted and cured.

presently out of hand in warlike sorte at the charge of this towne unto whiche charge the whole north division being x hundred shd. be contrybutaries, a letter to the like effect came to the Earl of Bath & Mr. H. Fortescue for the rating the country, and the counsel appointed George Pyne Maior of this towne. Mr. Thomas Leigh and Bartholomew Harrys for the purveyrs for the vict[u]als & other charge of the ship.

—By the Earl of Baths letter and order there was appoynted to be layd out by this town forthwith one hundred pounds by [South] Molton forty pounds by Torrington £xv and by Bediford [Bideford] £xx, and a meetyng at this time by divers of the said townes who agreed and made proporcon of the charge thereof for five months to be nyne hundred pounds & above, this charge was both for the victualling the xl men that shd. go in said shipp, for their wages and the wag[e]s of the shipp & other necessaries.[133]

1596.

—came to the Key head an old shipp of Mr. John Delfrigs called the Busse of Cxx Tun to rip[pe]d abroad.

An. 1596. On Monday being the 3d of ['May' crossed through] *May by vertue of the new charter of the libertyes of this towne, ther was kept at the Guyldhall a Sessions being the first that ever was kept within this towne.*

76—3 May a sessions held at the Guildhall the first after the new charter & the first ever kept in the town.

—In the beginning of this month May divers salt petre makers with commission to enter into houses & places to dig & delve upp the earth to make the peter, and do make salt peter thereof and clear salt, they take the earth dug up and cast water thereunto & so standeth a certain tyme then they let the water out of the tubb and by a certain tyme after boyl the same in a great furnace a long tyme then they take it out and put in small vessels to cowle [cool], and thereof cometh the salt peter & salt.

133. The Privy Council instructed the town of Barnstaple to furnish a ship of war. The earl of Bath was to oversee that contributions were made by the surrounding parishes: *Acts of the Privy Council, 1595–6*, 272–3.

—All this May hath not been a dry day and night.[134]
77—4th June this year Robarte Gill, John Gill, John Gill [?sic] & Nicholas Furlong were disfranchised[135] for not paying their rates towards shyppynge of the Prudence, & for other dismeanors both in speach & otherwise.
—wheat at xs. rye at vii barley at vi ots @ iis iiiid.[136]
78—16 June Ann Kemyns, Nichs. Gay's daughter[137] and one Davy[138] were all carted about the town for their filthie and lascivious life and the next day being fryday they satt all three at the high cross in the stocks.[139]
79—my brother Nycholas Wyat Judg of the Admiralty.
—continual rains wheat @ xis rye vis iiid barley viis. iiii.[140]
81—8th August arrivd the Prudence which brought much pillage from takeying of Cales [Cadiz].
—By reason of the continual rain there is great leare[141] of all sorts of corn, but little comes to market.
—Wheat xis rye & barley viii oats iis. iiiid. whereupon upon letters sent from the counsels to Earl of Bath he with other justices came to town viewd the market and sat the prices upon corn there (to wit) wheat ixs. ry vis. barley vs. ots iis. threatning the seller with dures[s] if he sold for above that price.[142]
—same day pclamation made wch did concerne the rats & taxations of servants waigs made by the justices of the peace for this Borough of Barnestaple, &c.
81—small Quantitie of corn brought to market townsmen cannot have corn for money.

134. There was probably generation apprehension over prices at this time; on 3 May forty 'brewsters and tipplers' were cited for acting contrary to the law: NDRO, B1/46/374.
135. Disenfranchised, they were deprived of their civil and electoral privileges.
136. The copy the Lysons saw has these same prices: Lysons, *Magna Britannia*, 32.
137. In 1584–5 Nicholas Gay and his 'whore' were carted in the town: Chanter and Wainwright, *Reprint*, II, 111.
138. In 1586–7 one 'Davies' maid was whipped twice: Chanter and Wainwright, *Reprint*, II, 111.
139. The three each had an illegitimate child born. William Keyninge was baptized on 6 June 1592, Arthur Davy (son of Mary) was baptized on 1 April 1593 and Emmet, daughter of Agnes Gaye, was baptized on 13 June 1593: NDRO, Barnstaple parish register.
140. The copy which the Lysons brothers examined noted that wheat was priced at 11s and barley at 7s 4d: Lysons, *Magna Britannia*, 32.
141. Presumably he meant a shortage.
142. The Lysons copy noted the same prices except for oats which was 5s: Lysons, *Magna Britannia*, 32.

82—upon Letters to Mr. Maior of this town from Mr. Norrys & Mr. Martyn in London mentioning the Dearth and Scarcity of Rye & price thereof that no less than a whole Shipps Quantity was to be had conteyning vii hundred quarters.

—Mr. Maior & his brethren had a Meeting thereon who debated but upon the wyllyngness of Mr. Nicholas Downe & John Delbridge they were all wyllyng to p[ro]cure a whole shipps lading, [marginal note] divers consented to lend £x wch extended to xii hundred pounds, George Stanbury, of this towne was appointed to travayl to London to assist Mr. Norrys in obtaining this corne; God speed him well that he may p[ro]cure some Corne for the Inhabitants of this Towne in this Time of Scarcity, that there is but little cometh to the Market & such snatching & catchying for that little and such a cry that the leke [like] was never heard,

which cost xiiii hundred pounds

—People which do wante seede do pay xii shillings for a bushel of wheat and much ado to geate it.[143]

83—came to the Custom house a stay for shippying with a Commandment from the Privy Counsellers to advtise them of number of Maryne[r]s and Shippynge with their Burdens belonging to Barnstaple.

84—not a dry Day in November.

—only Barley brought to Town & snatchd up presently[144]—300 Soldiers in the Town to go to Ireland.[145]

85—many of the Gentlemen shewd their light horses & petronells[146] in this Town before the Earl of Bath and Mr. Lewes Pollard their Captayn.

—Mr. Robert Appley one of the Maisters dyed and was buried in his own Tomb ['adjo' crossed through] in the Churchyard adjoining the South Wall of the Church, which he p[ro]cured a little while before his Death—he had been iii times Maior and all his tyme was earnest in

143. The Lysons' copy has the exact wording from 'Upon Letters to Mr Mayor' to 'much ado to get it' except for the use of the word 'coming' for 'cometh' and 'like' for 'leke': Lysons, *Magna Britannia*, 32.

144. The Lysons' copy had these two sentences exactly: Lysons, *Magna Britannia*, 32.

145. On 11 October the Queen wrote to the earl of Bath instructing him to levy 300 men in Devon for service in Ireland: *CSPD 1595–1597*, 292–3; Barnstaple had been a port of embarkation for Ireland for many years: *CSPD 1581–1590*, 16, 92. See also *CSPD 1595–1597*, 404.

146. Petronel: a large pistol or carbine.

upholding the Liberties of this Towne, and had been often Burgess of parliament—left considerable Lands in Barnstaple & Newport.[147]
—['to be produce of Barnestaple Lands to be layd out by the Maior and Aldermen Barnestaple lands' crossed through] the Maior and Aldermen to receive the Profitts untill it do amount to the Sum of one hundred pounds to be lent to poor Artificers[148] upon good Security after the one hundred pounds levyed the Lands to remain to the Corporacon.
—Newport Lands to be received by Maior & Aldermen for [illegible crossed through]ii poor people in Almslane to be divided.
86—Intelligence from Norrys and Stanbery that they had bought a Quantity of Rye & that the Justices of Peace having set a price upon corn, now gave leave to the Country to sell at large.
—hoping the Market w[oul]d be thereupon supplied but there cometh less & less & they aske xvs a b[ushe]l for wheat & comonly sell for xiis & vis & viiis for Barley.[149] [slip of paper attached to top of page. Cometh to Marke ... Wheat 12s Barley 6/8]
—continual Rain day & night.
—In the Christmas there was delivered unto his Honor (E. of B.) by Mr. Maior & the Aldermen a patent under their common seal of the Office of Recorder of this Towne, wche his Honor did willyngly accepte.
—Mr. John Trender, Vicar of this Town,[150] inveighd in his Sermon ag[ains]t the Aldermen for not coming to Church whom he said were like 2 fat Oxen that they would not hear when X [Christ] calld unto them but drew backwards and drew others from X, the aldermen were present but unseen for this and his indecent Behaviour on being questiond for this abuse he was committed towardes for want of Sureties—the E. of Bath next day dischargd him..
—William Collibear sen. Adlman, who during his Office is a Justice

147. He was buried on 28 November 1596: NDRO, Barnstaple parish register.
148. One who works by art or skill.
149. The Lysons' copy repeats this passage exactly from 'Intelligence' to 'for barley': Lysons, *Magna Britannia*, 33.
150. John Trynder was instituted 12 September 1593 and died November 1628. His memorial states 'Many are the troubles of the righteous, but the Lord delivereth them out of all': J.R. Chanter, *Memorials of St Peter's Church Barnstaple*, 95–6.

was bound over by E. of Bath and Mr. H. Ackland to appear at the next sessions [in pencil. of Barum] for behaviour.
—The like was never heerd before it was all Mr. Ackland's doinge who prevaild on E. of Bath to join him in it.
92—Mr. Downe & Delbridge Burgesses of this Towne,[151] purchasd. a quantitie of Rie & sold it @ ixs the Bushel to the Poore.
—Wheat sells for xiiii a b[ushe]l., and oten malt @ iiis. & viii, Barley @ ixs.
—the Justices of the Countrye levyed Contributions on the Parishes and C pounds was raised in this Town to send to Dansick [Danzig] for Rie.[152]

1597.
—8 April Wheat sold for xviiis. a b[ushel]l., Barley xiii, Rye xiiiis, Ots iiiis.
—10[153] June Wheat sold for xviii, Barley for xii, Rie for xvs. pr. bl.
—arrivd three shippes that were sent from hence to Dansick with Rie.

An. 1597. by reason of the cold, windy and rayny weather in the later end of July, the harvest is much backed, and the price of corn doth increase, so that, wheat was sold this last Fryday in July for 20s. the busshell and upwards. this was the dear year.

—now in Julye by reason of continual Raine Wheat sold last friday for xxs a bl.[154]

The 24th of Sept. Mr Thomas Hinson ['and' crossed through] *and Bartholomew Harris were elected burgesses for the Parliamt to be holden the 29th. of october next coming. Afterwards, because ther was some misliking by the Earle of Bath, of the choice of Bartholomew Harris to joyn with Mr Hinson, a new election was made by the consent of the*

151. Henry Downe was the son of Richard Downe of Barnstaple and born in 1536. He married Cicily Jewell of East Down. Delbridge was presumably John Delbridge, Barnstaple merchant and later Member of Parliament. There was no session this year. Perhaps Wyatt intended to write 'merchants': Drake, 'Members', 257; Grant, *Atlantic Adventurer*.

152. The Lysons' copy repeats the lines from 'Mr Downe' to 'barley at 9s' exactly and adds 'The justices of the county raised contributions to send to Dantzic for rye': Lysons, *Magna Britannia*, 33.

153. The Lysons' copy noted these same prices for an unspecified day in April except for oats which was priced at 4s 10d: Lysons, *Magna Britannia*, 33.

154. The Lysons' copy noted rye was priced at 15s and repeats the same lines from 'arrived three ships' to 'for 20s a bushel': Lysons, *Magna Britannia*, 33.

whole burgesses and therupon George Peard[155] *of this towne was made a free burgesse of this towne and then imediately* ['elected' inserted] *for one of the burgesses of the Parliamt in the Roome of Mr Harris and so Mr Hinson and Mr Peard*[156] *were returned for the two burgesses for this towne.*

—Thomas Hynson & Bartholomew Harris chosen Burgesses in Parliamt.[157]
[note]—afterwards there was some mislyking by the E. of Bath of the choice of B. Harrys to join with Mr. Hynson for one of the Burgesses of Parliament, a new Election was made by the Consent of the whole Burgesses, & George Peard of this Town was made a free Burgess of this town and then elected and returned with Mr. Hynson.
—Wheat xs., Rie ixs., Ots iis.

96—['Mr. Robert Bassett Capt. of the' crossed through] Traynd ['Bands' crossed through] Souldiers of Barnest. Pylton [Pilton] & Braunton[158] mustered before Mr. Robert Basset their Captn.[159]

98—Richard Symons Mr. of Arts was admytted Skolemr [schoolmaster] of this Towne & the other Symons was put out.[160]

1598.
3d. Aprill the towne of Tyverton [Tiverton] was adventurd with fyre began at the Wester End burnt the most part of the Town began about 1 in the Afternoon and before 5 all was brent and but a small part of their Goods savd many Men & Women burnt, CCCC houses & CCC pair of Lombes [looms], being Market day much Corn, Apples, butter & Cheese & market horses with abundance of Kersies,[161] the

155. George Peard was the son of John Peard, Barnstaple chamberlain: Haslam, *House of Commons*, III, 191–2.
156. Peard, son of John Peard of Barnstaple, married Agnes Jewell of East Down: Drake, 'Members', 257.
157. The summons date was 23 August and the sessions were 24 October to 20 December 1597 and 11 January to 9 February 1598.
158. The Braunton churchwarden accounts show training at Torrington but not Barnstaple: NDRO, 1677A/PW1A.
159. The town paid ten shillings for a banquet for Bassett at the 'first training of soldiers within the town': Wainwright, *Reprint*, II, 122.
160. For discussion of schoolmasters see David Cressy, 'A Drudgery of Schoolmasters: the Teaching Profession in Elizabethan and Stuart England', in Prest, *The Professions in Early Modern England*, 129–53.
161. Tiverton became wealthy at the end of the sixteenth century through the making of kersies, the coarse narrow woollen cloth.

Report goeth that the rich Men of the Town were unmercifull to the poor and sufferd them to dye in the Streets for want and so it might be *Digitus Dei.*[162]

[attached sheet to top of page. 1598 W 8 B 5]—Corn is fallen Wheat viii Rye vis Barley 5s. Ots xxiid.[163]

101—18 Aug. Richard Beaple elected a common Council Man in Room of Roger Cade who was put out for that he dwelld out of this Town above one year.

—27 dwelling Houses burnt at Great Torrington.[164]

104—Mr. Chechester, of Youlston kept his Audit in this Town.

—xxii decebr dyed my bro[the]r John Wyat at Braunton & buried in his yeld.[165]

An. 1598. The beginning of december this year the old shambles under the Guild-hall the postes and all were plucked downe and the place paved and a new bench set up by the ['m' crossed through] *norther wall and so it is appointed for a walking place.*

It is reported for certaine that our English souldiers carry over with ['them' crossed through] *them into Ireland great store of Buldogs*[166] *to be imployed upon the enemy.*

—beginning of Decr. the old Shambels under the Guildhall the posts and all were pluckd down and the place pavd and a new Bench set by the North Wall & so tis appoynted for a walkying place.[167]

105 In Innocents Week the Maior with many of his Brethren went to Youlston to visit Mr. Robart Chichester & carryd unto him some good Hansel,[168] they did the same to Mr. Bassets and also to Tawstock.

---

162. On 27 April the County Justices ordered that the 300 residents affected by the fire be given assistance by a general collection throughout the county. A number of the poor of Tiverton were sent to Barnstaple to be housed. On 4 October 1599 all those that were accommodated outside of Tiverton were ordered to remain there for another year. The town suffered another fire in 1612: DRO, QS/OB 1, 210–11, 285; Wainwright, *Reprint*, II, 131, 134.
163. The Lysons' copy repeated the same information for corn prices except for giving barley the price of six shillings: Lysons, *Magna Britannia*, 33.
164. On 3 April 1600 the County Justices ordered that the sum of £30 be given because of the 28 houses which were destroyed: DRO, DQS/OB/1, 314.
165. Aisle.
166. Most probably the cannon or small firearm then in use.
167. Walking place: a promenade.
168. Handsel: the custom of giving gifts expressing good wishes at the beginning of the New Year.

1599.

106—2 April Mr. Robert Chichester, Lord of this Towne beying advertysd of some Injuries done him by this Town came hyther with Mr. Hugh Wyet Lawyer & Counseller and the Counsel of this Town compromisd the Varyance.[169]

—this Month of Maye was the Enterclose and the little house in the Guildhall drawne downe the same hall enlarged, & the Wyndow of the same glassed.

108—xxix May one John Symons a petie Skolemaster of this Town not very hardly witted, but one of the Anabaptistical & Precise Brethren had a Child brought to the Church to be christend & calld it Doe well, the Vicar dislyking it calld it John, which caused a great murmuring among the Brethren who said it came from the Hebrew word Abdeel.

—xvth June Ld. Bathe & other justices had a conference here and after debatyng they concluded upon having a house of correction at Chumleigh within the North Division.

—The Countess of Baths Barque arrivd with much Merchendize of the Merchants of this Towne.

—A better Harvest never heard of than this[170] Wheat iiiis Barley iis. vid.

110—Earl of Bath Mr. Fortescue & Mr. Hugh Ackland sat concernyng rating of the Subsidy.

111—Wheat iii/iiiid Rye ii/viid Barley 2i[sic]/iiiid.[171]

—Certain Inhabitants of this Town which are no Burgesses [freemen] (viz) pentecost Dodderidge John Welsh, William Dawkyns, John Garret being rated for b[u]ying & selliyg & opening the Shop wyndows .... to the ancyente custome of this Towne refused to pay their rates, wch the Resceyver of this Towne took distresses from them for the same and thereupon the said Dodderidge sent immediately for a writ & arrested the Resceyver, who presently put in baile for his apparence at this michaelmas Term.

169. 'Comprised the variance', they had attempted to resolve the dispute.
170. This contrasts with the report of the earl of Bath to the Privy Council of 17 August that poor weather had damaged the harvest: PRO, SP12/272/51.
171. The Lysons' copy repeated the same prices for grain and noted the harvest with the same words: Lysons, *Magna Britannia*, 33.

Recusants[172] combyned together to try this Matter wth the Towne—the Mayor & his Brethren sent to the Earl of Bath who came to Town the xxvii day of November—sat at the Guildhall with Mr. Maior the Aldermen & whole Counsell—Dodderidge & Darracott appeared—then Mr. Thomas Leigh one of the learned Counsell of this Town opend the Case setting forth their abuses towards the Town to the breach of their Liberties & other offences wch were pved before his Honour—Dodderidge alledgd he was rated too much—his Honour told him he shd have applyd to him beynge Recorder—dodderidge replied he shd have done it but that a hundred of the Inferior sort w[oul]d have attended hym & thereby gyven his Hon. a deal of Trouble—Mr. Leigh tooke Advantage of this, how that he went to raise a Tumult & insurrection in the Town—whereupon his Honour commytted Dodderidge & Darracot to prison.

—After dinner his honr & Mr. Maior & common Counsell went again to the Guildhall Dodderidge & Darracott being sent for sentence was gyven against them (viz) that Dodderidge should be sent again to prison till he found Sureties for his good Behavr & hymself bound in C to her Majesty for his appearance before the Lds of her Majesty's Privy Counsell the vi of Feb. next followyng—Darracot to remayne in prison vi days & be bound to his good Behaviour & to appear at the next Assizes for Devon.

—Welsh appeard & standing stout he was requyrd to take the Oth and to be sworne as Censer [censure] for his Allegyance wch he refusing was commytted to prison.

—the thursday following Dodderidge entred into all the Recognizances & was released.

—after vi days Imprisonment upon Submission ['Welsh' crossed through] Darracot was dismyssed and so was John Welsh, but by what reason I knowe not so that the most part of this Mettal in the refyning went off in Smoke.

—xxiii december. this year a violent tempest of wynde—Stone coal[173] sold for ixd a bushel and a load of faggots & wood for xxd.

172. Recusants, those, particularly Roman Catholics, who refused to attend services of the Church of England.

173. Coal from South Wales.

113—xxvi day of January Mr. Thomas Leigh & Bartt. Harris began their Journey towards London on Ttownes behalf to psecute the Cause ag[ains]t Pentacost before the Counsel, carrying with them the new Charter and some of oure ..... with the booke of the Composition & divs. other Evidences & Records touching our ancyent custom now in Question.
—xxviii Jan. Mr. Maior resceyvd Orders from Lords of Counsell to p[ro]vide Shyppinge for transporting 200 Soldiers into Ireland.[174]
—If Soldiers stayd any Time p[ro]vision of vid a day for their Meat and the other ii to carry in theyr purses.
—wednesday xx feb Mr. Tho. Leigh & Harris returned with this Order that Dodderidge shd pay the xxd he was sette and to be made a Burgese of this Towne paying £1 as others doe.

1600.

114—Monday the xix day of Maye the new Kaye [quay] upon the strand, almost in the midst of the other Kay was begun to be buylded.
—xi Augt. John Delbridge mercht. elected Maior.[175]
—on this Day William Collibeare who had been Maior ii tymes of this towne, for that he had by the Space of ii yeres or above dwelt out of towne & now set out his howse in Towne where he dwelt & so no hope of his returne to Towne agayne and was dismyssed of his room in the common Counsell of this Towne & disfranchysed &c. and immediately thereupon William Shapleigh was elected in his roome & sworne &c.
—This yere at the Request of Sr. Robert Bassett one Sharland[176] a musician was retaind by Mr. Maior & his Brethren to go about the Town about iiii oclock in the Morning with his waits[177] & is promisd £viii—began on all saints day [31 October] & to continue till candlemas [2 February].

174. At this time the parish of Hartland paid eleven shillings and nine pence towards the costs: Ivon L. Gregory, *Hartland Church Accounts, 1597–1706* (Frome and London, 1950), 19.
175. Delbridge appears to have been an effective mayor: Grant, *Atlantic Adventurer*, 14–18; Delbridge regarded Thomas Hinson, steward at Tawstock to the Earl of Bath, as his enemy: *CSPD 1601–1603*, 200.
176. In 1609–10 Sherland was paid £4 for his wages: Wainwright, *Reprint*, II, 118.
177. Wait: watchman.

—Order in Towne that the Maister & other of the common Counsell shd hang out Candles & Lanterns at their doors in dark nights in the wynter till ix oclock.
—This November the loft over the Kayhall was new planchd & repaird in order to make a Bridewell.[178]
117—Friday xiv novr. Mr. Maior & aldermen going upon their Search in the evenyng as usuall found the vicar Mr. Trynder in John Williams House being a tipler wth. other Company and having amongst them a pipe with a Taber[179] a little after nyne, & because Mr. Trynder wd. not come down to Mr. Maior from the Chamber upon commandment & for other his ...... was commytted to warde where he abode till .... mornynge followying, in the mean tyme
118 he sent a lamentable lre [letter] to the Bp of Exeter[180] advtising his Ldp that he was wrongfully commytted & without any Cause, whereupon his Ldp wrote to E. of Bath—who commanded the Maior to come to him wch. he did at Tawstock—a day appointed for hearing—vicar releasd—sunday following he preachd ii hours beinge a cold daye he weryed all his audience.
—tuesday following it was heard & determind that there was just cause for his being detaynd & to be bound for his good behavr yet Mr. Maior by his Hons. pswasion, & his own concern remytted to my Lord of Baths censure.
—Butler was schoolmaster.
119—Orders for shippynge for transporting 150 soldyrs to Kyngsale [Kinsale].
—Mr. Richard Smyth the hired preacher of this town[181] & Jo: Smyth preacher of Pylton [Pilton] were inhibited to preach in this Dioces by reason they wd. not wear the Surplice.
120—In hillary Mr. Trynder the vicar was pcepted to appear before the high Commssioners in matters ecclesiastical to answer Articles

178. The sum of £4 14s 6d was paid by the town for the improvements and repairs of the house of correction: NDRO, B1/3972/162.
179. Two musical instruments: the tabor was a small kind of drum commonly used to accompany the pipe.
180. William Cotton who died 26 August 1621.
181. In 1600 Smith was paid £4 as his annual stipend: Wainwright, *Reprint*, II, 99. He was the author of *A Munition against Man's Misery and Mortality* (1610).

exhibited by Richard Ley (but by the instence of Mr. Maior and others of this Towne)
—so there is no liklihood of good government while such Dissencons last.
—at the Assizes at Exeter before Mr. Justice Wamsley & Mr. Justice Venner xviii psoners recd. sentences & were executed.

1601.

An ['1601' crossed through] *1601* ['on' inserted] *Thursday being the 22 of october, the wife of Walter Jones of this towne brough fourth a child* ['and' crossed through, 'wch' inserted] *was baptized and then she stayed untill the Sonday following, and then she brought fourth another child, but it* ['wa' crossed through] *was dead borne.*[182]

121—Smyth allowd to preach agayne, & did preach & admynyster the Communion in his surples as he was commanded.
—xxv of Aprill orders to take up Shyppynge for 150 soldiers.
—The Sessions & the Law Court of this towne were kept this yere the iii day of May 1601. Mr. John Delbridge Maior being absent in Northamptonshire or London on business[183]—no dinner kept at Maior's house for maisters, steward or otherwise—towards Expence of dinner the Jury had each vid & the Town clerke viiid.
—This order hath no father to any Man's remembrance now living but spronge up of the infected ayr lately amongst us.
—the jury save one dynd at William Clyverdons & adding to their Allowance they spent ixd apeece & had good cheer with wyne, &c
G. Stanbury elected maior.
—Corne continud this yere nere one rate.
123—Wheat v/iiiid. Rye iiii/iiiid Barley iii/viiid[184]
—Mr. Maior returning from London brought letters that ['ii thousand' crossed through] souldyers wd. be transported to Ireland.[185]

182. The baptism of Joseph the son of Walter Jones was recorded for 22 October 1601: NDRO, Barnstaple parish register.
183. NDRO, B1/3972/162. The Received also noted the Mayor's absence.
184. The Lysons' copy also had these prices: Lysons, *Magna Britannia*, 33.
185. The town spent £4 3s 8d in May and £3 13s 4d for the soldiers in August: NDRO, B1/3972/162.

—p[ro]visions & shyppyng to be p[ro]vided for them accordingly—450 for dublyn [Dublin], & 975 for Waterford viz. Cornwall 100, devon 300, dorcet [Dorset] 100, Somerset 250, Wilts[hire] 125, Southampton 100.
—775 Souldyers in this town at one tyme.[186]
125—xxxi October Ser Anthony Cook Knyght came to conduct the Souldyers to Ireland.
126. Edward Handcocke Esquyre and Richard Martyn born in Exeter & of the inner Temple in London are Burgesses at the new Parliamt for this town of Barnestaple,[187] the first appoynted by the Earl of Bath & the other by Mr. Robert Chechester of Youlston who at this tyme had the nomination of them both.[188]
—xix day of december at night some of the Castle wall was blown down & blown into the Castle & did no harme savying some ii Ravens were found dead & beleke sat within side the wall.
—650 Souldyers to be transported into Ireland from hence & p[ro]vision made accordingly.
127. Mr. Butler, the schoolm'. inhibited from teaching till shews by what Authority he teaches.[189]
—The Bp. of Exeter sent a schoolmr. Mr. Mansfield.

on Christmas day last past is most certenly reported by such as were at it that the Lord Dep. of Ireland not far from Corke meeting the Earl of Terone [Tyrone] in the field gave him an overthrow & killed 1500, took many prysoners & 5 Auncyents 11 of the Spanish & 11 of the Irish, but the Earl escaped, whereupon shortly after Don Juan de Argala [Juan d'Aguila], Chief & general of the Spaniards (by composition) gave up Kingsale [Kinsale] and many other places & had leave to hire shippynge & go away.

186. From 1 November 1601 to 14 February 1602 there were burials for 8 soldiers recorded from Somerset, Wells and Northampton: NDRO, Barnstaple parish register.
187. Hancock was the son of William Hancock of Combe Martin and married Dorothy Bampfylde of North Molton. He was Clerk of the Assizes and Recorder of Exeter. Hancock died in about 1616. Martyn was the son of William Martyn of Exeter and born in about 1570. He became barrister-at-law of the Middle Temple in 1602 and in 1618 was appointed Recorder of London. He died that year: Drake, 'Members', 258.
188. The summons date was 11 September and the sessions dates were 27 October to 19 December 1601.
189. In 1601–2 six shillings and eight pence was paid to John Norrys for his expenses in travelling to the bishop regarding the schoolmaster: Wainwright, *Reprint*, II, 114.

1602.

129—the Assizes at Exeter held in March, before Ld. Chief Baron Pencim[190] & Justice Venner—no psoners condemned nor executed—altho in the Gaol were many for notorious crimes but by Report the Lord ch[ief]. B[aron]. mynde extended to the Pecution[191] of the recusants for he sent to the common gaol Mr. Giles Risdon & Mr. William Burgoyne being recusants there to remayne at his pleasure—if they had rather go to Goal then to Church much good myght it doe them. I am not of theyr Myndes.[192]

An. 1602

Upon tuesday the 18th day of May the Earle of Bath and ['other' crossed through] *diverse Justices of the peace having sate heer about mustering and pressing souldiers for Ireland. the said Earle and Justices dined with Mr Maior upon a* ['Scarbo' crossed through] *Skarborough warning, as I did hear.*[193]

—200 Souldyers sent to Ireland from hence.
—great Thunder & lightenynge in June the beacon of Mattynhoe [Martinhoe] was brent.

An. 1602. the 9th day of August Mr Bartholomew Harris was elected maior of this town of Barum for the year following and it was then agreed and concluded by the comon counsell that the maior of this year, and so the former maior heerafter continually shall be the elder Alderman for the year following, wherupon Mr George Stanberie the now maior was chosen for one of the Aldermen for the year following.

—ix of Augt. Mr. Barth. Harris chosen Maior & then agreed that the old Maior shall be the elder Alderman.

190. Sir William Peryam, judge of the common pleas from 1581.
191. Prosecution.
192. At the Quarter Sessions on 15 April 1602 the justices bound over a number of recusants. They included Elizabeth Risdon, the wife of the above-mentioned Giles Risdon of Parkham, gentleman: DRO, DQS/OB/2, 15 April 1602 [no page numbering].
193. A very short notice or no notice at all.

131—about the End of this August came to Towne one Edward Abbotts that xii. yere paste did leeve with Mr. Robert Prowze of this towne & during the service came acquainted with Elizabeth Morcombe of this place who pmised each other Marriage—he went to live in London afterwards with ['merchant' crossed through] Alderman Spencer who sent him in Trade unto the Streights of Aleppo [Gibraltar].
—he renewed his old love & they were marrid at wch. were present Ld. Bath & the Countess, Mr. Seymor & many other from the Southams [South Hams]—he was supposed to be the bere[194] son of old Ld. Edward Seymor of Berryepomeroy [Berry Pomeroy]—he is accounted to be worth iiii or v thousand pounds.[195]
135.—Wheat holdeth up at viii/viiiid a bushel, Rye at vi/iiiid, Barley vs, ots xxiid.[196]

An. 1603. The masons began the wals of the new-worke upon the key, the monday being the 6th of June, and that day the great dornes[197] of the gate were set up.

1603.

6 June. The Masons began the walls of the new works & that Day the great Dorns of the Gate were sat up.
—many Barks and Trous[198] of corn from the forest arrivd here.

3 Feb. pclamation publishd concerning Election of Knyghts of the Shire & Burgesses for Parliamt. that they shd. be grave men, of good worthe & fit for the place.
136—Merchants & Shippes belonging to this Towne go & traffick [trade] into Spain & Portugal as usual.
137. In this Hillary Term Mr. John Dodderidge .... in this Towne & hath been Maior twice .... a Serjeant of the Lawe, & the younge ...... the Taylr. that br[ough]t his new Robe unto h ...... house at

194. Presumably the illegitimate son.
195. Edward Abbott and Elizabeth Morcombe were married on 20 September 1602: NDRO, Barnstaple parish register.
196. The Lysons' copy had the same prices: Lysons, *Magna Britannia*, 33.
197. Durn, the framework of a doorway.
198. Trow, the large flat-bottomed barge used on the Severn.

London the same day was buryed in ...... dayes following, wch. broughte some feare ..... those that sat with hym at Dynner that day ....

1604.

—friday 24 feb. Mr. Thomas Hinson, Esq. was sworne a free Burgess. ['—Saturday 25 Feb. was elected with Mr George Peard Gent. for this B' crossed through]

xxv of februarie then followyng the said Mr. Thomas Hinson & George Pearde gent. were elected & chosen for two Burgesses of this Towne to be at the foresaid p[ar]liam—t. in Behalf of this Towne.[199]

An. 1604. Ther hath this spring time been brought to this towne by water from diverse places great quantitie of wheat, Barley, Pooles[200] *and barley-malt about the quantity of twenty thousand busshels and far above by good account, wherby the price of such grayne is much mitigated what otherwise it would have been. The price of corne in* ['february' crossed through] *July was 6s. 8d. the busshell of wheat, and in the winter before about 6s.*[201]

—The plague entred into this Countrye[202]—Great Quantitie of Wheat barley pooles & Barley malt about xx thousand bushels.
—Wheat vi viii Rye vs Barley iii/viiid.[203]
—xxviii prisoners executed at Exeter this Summer assize before Justice Venner and Warberton.

199. Parliament was summoned 31 January and the sessions dates were 19 March to 7 July 1604, 5 November 1605 to 27 May 1606, 18 November 1606 to 4 July 1607, 9 February to 23 July 1610 and 16 October to 6 December 1610.

200. Possibly oats.

201. The Lysons brothers noted for 1664, which was probably an error for 1604, that 'about the beginning of March, wheat was sold in the market for 4s 10d and 4s 8d, but in a fortnight after it was sold for 7s 6d occasioned by engrossing: Lysons, *Magna Britannia*, 33.

202. There was disease at Exeter, Barnstaple, Great Torrington and Kingswear in 1604: DRO, DQS OB 1/2, Pas. 1604, OB 1/3, fo. 145; Also on 14 April 1607 the justices at the Quarter Sessions enquired into the plague formerly at Barnstaple: DRO, DQS OB 1/2. Thirty-four plague deaths were recorded with a 'p' next to their names in the parish register with the first on 13 November and the last on 15 April 1605. They included two children in the 'pest house': NDRO, Barnstaple parish register; Also this year the town made a collection for those 'sick of the plague' at Ilfracombe. In Barnstaple the sum of six shillings and three pence was expended 'for the provision of divers that were willed to keep themselves into their houses in Crock Street upon suspicion that the plague had been amongst them': NDRO, B1/3972/164.

203. The Lysons' copy had the same prices: Lysons, *Magna Britannia*, 33.

139—This October the Deputy of his Majesty's Clerk of the Market came about this Countrey & made lesse all bushels pecks and half-pecks by the third part ['after' crossed through in pencil] ['of the' added in pencil] Winchester bushel. countenancd by the Justices of the peace to the great Admiracon of many & is thought to be a great Grief.[204]

And so now our clerke of the Market being Henry Downe followeth the like fashion within this Towne

140—in the beginning of this November the plague entred into this towne—few dyed—many died at Torrington.[205]

141—on palm Sunday 24 daye of March dyed at Tawstock the Countes of Bath[206] & that night following she was buryed—but the Solemnization of her funeral was deferrd until some tyme afterwards.

1605.

—The Monday beyinge the vith day of Maye 1605 was the funeral of the late Elizabeth Countes of Bath solempnized at Tawstock there came down from London Three Deputie Harolds of Armes, the principal Mourner was the young Lady Frances Bowchier, and there were viii other murners of the poorer sort of the same p[ari]sh; Mr. Saunders the Earl of Bath's Chaplayne did preach that day; much meate & drinke eat & drank at Tawstock Court all the poor had iiid. a piece & loaf of bread.[207]

6 June was an Admiralty Court held in this Towne by the E. of Bath Vice Admiral concerning the new work because the said E. doth much envey ag[ains]t. it.[208]

204. 'The deputy of the King's clerk of the market came about the county, and caused all corn to be sold by the Winchester measure, countenanced by the justices of the peace, to the admiration of many, and thought to be a great grief': Lysons, *Magna Britannia*, 33.

205. Six shillings and three pence were spent in restraining a number of people suspected as diseased from leaving houses in Crock Street: Chanter and Wainwright, *Reprint*, II, 132.

206. Eight pence was paid to the watchman on the bridge this day: Chanter and Wainwright, *Reprint*, II, 133; She was buried on the 25th of March: NDRO, Tawstock parish register.

207. The parish register confirms that she was buried on the 6th of May: NDRO, Tawstock parish register.

208. There are recurrent entries in the borough accounts regarding the work on the quay. For 1604–5 there is one entry of a payment of 23 shillings for 'the town clerk for drawing and engrossing in answer to the articles exhibited unto the Earl of Bathon against this town by the bargemen and others concerning the new work upon the quay and drawing down thereof and for divers other writing by him made touching the town's business there this year, as appears by the particulars thereof': NDRO, B1/3972/164.

142—Mr. Nicholas Wyat as Judg of the Admiralty of Devon, kept the court, Mr. Bridgman's Son being notary—Mr. Hugh Ackland & Mr. Hinson sat in the court in the Morning & my Ld. of Bath in the Afternoon when the Jury gave up the Verdict which was that it was noysome to passage of boats & barges.
—Mr. Bar. Harris John Norris Jas. Downe were all 4 indicted for building the new work—supposing the same to be Annoyance to Boats.[209]

12 Augt. James Woodrough was elected Maior—before the Election he prevaild on 15 to promise that they wd. not ballot for him, but they disceivd him & he was chosen—he was absent & had appointed his Voice & Ball unto Robert Honey.[210]
144—About the Middle of the Month of Augt. the Earl of Bathon Sr. Ro. Chichester Sr. Hen. Roll & Mr. Hugh Ackland sat in the Guildhall by Virtue of certain Orders from the Counsell to meet about alehouses Drunkers, recusants &c—a great Cry and little wool.[211]

1606.

17 May John Sallesbury elected a common Counsel man in the room of Wm. Shapleigh who dwelleth at Bideford & did dwell out of this Town above one yere & a day and therefore loosing his Freedom & Libtie that he had in Town he was likewise dismyssd of his ['Gowne' crossed through] Roome.
—The Monday Mornying tide beyinge as faire weather and as calme as may be two of the Dukes of Tawton havynge laden sande at the Rudge ag[ains]t Castle Point, and upward bound did strike the Bridge & sunke and one other boat laden with sande comynge short after them and beyng is some danger in that she went oute over the barge that was sunk took up both men & escapd without damage.
—the reason of striking was the boatsmens making his Oar so stricte that he cod. stir the barge.

209. Mr Bartholomew Harris was paid thirty pounds for his expenses of the 'new works': Chanter and Wainwright, *Reprint*, II, 107. Further money was also expended by the town and finally some four years later the matter was resolved with a dinner to mark the occasion: NDRO, B1/3972/168–77.
210. The mayor was chosen by the council who each placed a ball in one of the two designated ballot pots.
211. Orders were received from the Privy Council at the county's quarter sessions dated 23 June. These included orders regarding wages, rogues, tipplers and recusants: DRO, DQS/OB/2, no page number.

Augt. Mr. John Peard elected Maior.
—the last Month the Lady Bassett[212] came to towne to dwell in Mr. Nichs. Downes new House upon the Kay.

xiii day of Septemb came Mr. John Dodderidge the King's solicitor and Mrs. Dorathy his Wife & staid here some daies with his father.
—This last Somer Assize came down for Judgs Ld. Chief Baron & Justice Tanfild at wch Assize Sr. Roberte Chichester had a Trial ag[ains]t the Towne for Gortons house by the Castlegreen, wch. passed wth Sr. Robert C. by reason of three witnesses wch. he brought (viz.) Philip Ley William Brooke & Richard Rise that did swear that the house did stand in the dike altho' it be most apparent that the same is fare withoute, and so verified at the Trial by the Oths of vii credible witnesses.
151—30th October 3 persons were apprehended two on Suspicion of counterfeiting iids another for stealing Cloaths—one of them digd a hole in the Prison Wall in got out into the Ch[urch]. yard.

An. 1606. ['The' crossed through] *On tuesday morning being the 20th day of January and upon the highest of the spring the winde blowing very hard at South-west, ther was such a flood or tide as the like was never seen in this towne. It come into all the houses and sellers neer the key with such a powre, that it burst open dores that were lockt and bolted, and threw downe many houses and wals, that this towne hath received losse in salt, sugar, oade*[213] *&c to the valew of one thousand pounds. In southgate street it came up above the plumpe,*[214] *also more then halfe way up Maiden street, in Crockstreet it came up so far as Mr Takels hall-doore: the tombstone upon the key was covered clean over with water by report of diverse: It threw down the whole house wherin one James Frost did dwell wherby himselfe was slayne with fall of the roofe, and his two children lying in their bed, were slayne with the fall of the wall upon them. This tide went clean over the Pilton*

212. She was visited by John Sweet, a suspected Catholic: HMC, *Salisbury*, XVIII (1940), 213, 252.
213. Woad: *Isatis tinctoria*, which yields a blue dye.
214. Pump.

bridge, and so shooke the wester wall therof, that it was moved three or fower ynches out from the cawsey [causeway] *and much of it ready to fall down &c. The water was higher at this tide by 5. or 6. foot then ever it was seen by any now living.*

—a very great floud—damage £1000—water came up in Southgate Street above the plump to the higher end of Thomas Harris house, and in Wilstreet upp that way untill the Widow Taylors window, it come to Appleys fore door & run out thro the house into the Garden there & made great spoyle.
—The water flowd up more than half way Mayden Street & then went into there houses.
—also it came upp at the lower end of Crockstreete so far Mr. Takles hall door.
—The Tombstone upon the Kaye was coverd clene over with water—by report it was higher by v or vi foote than ever remembred by those now lyvinge.
—First to digresse westward from the Kaye it threw down a great part of the utter[215] wall of Mr. Collybears house—it cast down the easter[n] wall of Mr. Dodderidges Courtledge upon the Kaye.
—it had almost cast down a little House of Mr. Stanberie's standynge there in the east part of the Kay, but it brused it soe that they were dryven to draw it down for fear of falling & make it upp agayne.
—It threw down the whole house whereon James Frost did dwell whereby himself was slayn with the fall of the roofe & two Children lying within bed were slayn with the falling of the Walls.[216]
—All the walls between that and the Castle fell and the top of the house of the horse Mill began to cleave asunder & likely to have fallen down if the Spill[217] of the Mill wch. was very strong had not supported it.

215. Outward or further.
216. The parish register records the deaths of James, Sabine and Catherine Frost on 20 January 'with the fall of their house': NDRO, Barnstaple parish register.
217. Possibly spile: a wooden post.

—it cast down divers walls in Litchdon—it hurted all the walls on the Kay next the River.[218]

1607.

—Mr. Richd. Beaple elected Maior.

—Orders to the Maior to provide for 200 Soldyers for Ireland—100 whereof were Devonshire Men, who had their Conduct Money & Apparel (to wit) a Monmouth Capp[219] a Coate a Doublet ii shirtes a paire of breeches a paire of Stockinges a paire of Shoes, & vs in money.[220]

—about fortnight before Xmas began the hard frost wch. continued v weeks—the victuals bought in the market was so frosen it would take no salt.

158—The cold meat after it was dressd and kept one night was so hard that it could not be cut to be eaten for I had a piece of Beef that was roasted the Day before New Years day & kept it untill the thursday following and then was I driven to take a Spit and put the End thereof into the fire and heat it redd hot and so got him in the flesh & new rosted it by the Space of an hour & half before it was thorough hot & then usd the same.[221]

160—Last Lent Mr. Harris & Mr. John Delbridge of this towne by Order and Consent of this Town exhibited a ['Complaint' crossed through] petition before the Lords in Counsell contayning a Complaint of the Maior Aldermen & Burgesses ag[ains]t. Mr. Hugh Acklande a Justice of Peace of divers enormities injuries and ill Demeanors by him daily commyted agt. the State and Government of the Towne, altho he had always among good entertainment of wch. Complaint the Lords takying due Consideracon wrote Lres [letters] to the Judges at Assizes

218. The Lysons brothers summarized this as '1606. A great flood; the damages estimated at £1000; by report five or six feet higher than ever was known by any living; several houses much damaged and some thrown down; in one house a man and his two children killed': Lysons, *Magna Britannia*, 34.

219. A flat round cap.

220. On 15 November the earl of Bath wrote to the earl of Salisbury that 'a great number of the most able men of the county, very meet for the service fled from home to avoid it' and that a great number of 'lusty tall fellows, volunteers and idle persons' had offered to go: HMC, *Salisbury*, XIX (1965), 326. Also see page 363.

221. The 'extreme frost' caused the lead pipes to freeze in Plymouth: WDRO, Widey Court Book, 1607; D. Quinn, A.M. Quinn and S. Hillier (eds), *New American World* (New York and London, 1979), III, 437.

to bind over Mr. Ackland to appear before their Ldps or end the Controversies.
161—the Judge receyving the Letters Mr. Ackland was calld before them & he told those that were present that the Counsell had a great regard of the town of Barns. that it had done divers Services as well to the late Gracious Queen as to his present most excellent Majesty in receyg. of Souldyers often tymes sent into Ireland, & therefore their Honours were to uphold the Rights—Then Sir John Ackland desired that he might have the hearing of the Causes in difference—wch. the Judg. objected to unless the Townsmen agreed thereto—but by the earnest Request of Sir John Ackland Mr. Maior & his Brethren commytted the whole Cause unto Sr. John Acklands hands, upon promyses that he & his Brother w[oul]d always hereafter bear good affection to the Towne & doe any thing for their good, the cause pceeded no farther.
—at the same the new worke was in Question & the Judges havyng receyvd Letters from Lords of Counsel were in a milder censure & Conceyt therewith, there was Mr. Hinson & Mr. Richard Ley & divers others followed the Cause ag[ains]t the Town & were earnest to Jdgmt wch shewd a plott[222] drawn of the new worke, the Judg being commanded to stop Judgmt & to take a view of the work—Viewers were appoynted by consent of all parties Sr. John Ackland Sr. Amias Bampfield Sr. Thomas Browne Sr. Henry Roll &c. elder knight. Mr. Anthony Monck, Mr. Arthur Harris & Mr. William Carie to view and to certify at next Assizes.
162—Wheat ix/iii Rye vii Barley vi.
—By reason of sharp cold winter hay sold for viii & ixs a truss.
—Many Cattle died for want of Fodder.
25 May. Mr. Maior recd. Letter by a pursuivant from the Counsel for appoynting a Stage Post from this Town to Chumleigh & a poste barke to carry any packet sent hether from my Lord Treasurer into the province of Munster in Irelande.[223]

222. See Map 4.
223. A messenger was given 6d by the town for bringing letters from the Privy Council regarding a postal service to Ireland: Wainwright, *Reprint*, II, 157.

An. 1607. On Tewsday being the 19th day of may between sixe and seven of the clock in the forenoone ther was a little earth-quake perceived and seen within this towne that both the earth and houses did quiver and shake, for a small time, yet no hurt done.

2 July the Knight & Gentlemen about the new worke met the greatest parte & did see the bargs pass the Bridge with sand who passd safe except one who struck on purpose.
—the Gent were Sr. Wm. Strode Mr. Seymor Sir Amias Bampfylde Sr. Thomas Browne Sr. Henry Rolle Mr. Anthony Monck Mr. Ar. Harris & Mr. William Cary—after view sat in Guildhall & heard the Bargmen—they spoke as they w[oul]d for they were not sworne.
—much ado at this Assizes about the new work, the adverse party pcurd the Judg to give his Verdict agaynst it—but it was not then entred.
167 friday the xiv of October, upon determinacon agreed by Mr. Maior &c. to remove the Cornmarket it was pclaimd in the same Market Place, Mr. Maior & the most part of the comon Counsel being present that the sd Corn Market shd be translated, & from thenceforth be kept in the North side of high street, beginning at Mr. Nichs. Downe's house & so northwarde.

An. 1607. the sixth day of december the Penelope a ship of this harbour of the burthen of 150 tonnes and upward having been this year at Newfoundland and Lisbone in her returne, ['was' crossed through] *stroke aground a mile within the bar on the souther side: the next day she lay upright and reasonable weather yet none of the company (who had upon her striking aground forsooke her and with her boat went ashore) would go* ['or stay' crossed through] *or stay aboard to make any shift for her but unloaded some part of her goods; so that the next tide shee was torne in pieces. Because she was a very tall ship, many factors[224] in Lisbone did send home in her diverse bags of mony; wherof diverse were embeaselled, and some they shared amongst them. The judgmt of most was that the money cast away the ship, because it was evident that the company might have saved her, if they listed.*

224. Factors: mercantile agents.

This year was the great frost for five weekes together, viz from ['fo' crossed through] *about fortnight before Christmas to the sonday after twelfe day* [6 January], *The water of Tawe both above and beneath the* ['bridge' crossed through] *bridge was frozen over and over. and I saw diverse to go down upon the ice in the midst of the chanell from the bridge to the castle point, and up upon the same againe to the bridge. The ground was so hard by the extremity of the frost, that the birds could get no meat, so that many dyed of famine and were so found dead in diverse places, that now at last ther were none left to be seen.*[225]

1608.

—new Indictmt ag[ains]t Mr. Bar. Harris John Norris James Down & others about the new work.
—Sheriff ordered to return 48 of the E. & S. Divisions & 24 to be drawn—many witnesses examined before the Lord Chief Baron.
—20 Apr. the Spire on the Keyhal [Quay Hall] was finishd.
170 At this Assize the xxxi day of Julye the Judges sat at one Bench—exceptions argud by Counsel—the Judges went to Launceston & the Indictees orderd to meet at Sr. John Ackland the Sherifs.
—after Conference had about the Matter Mr. Richard Harris Maior Mr. Richard Beaple Mr. Bartholemew Harris & others met at Crediton the adversaries Mr. Hinson Mr. Hugh Acland Richard Ley one Pearse an attorney Bar: Berry Thomas Loverynge & others, but never a lawyer for so the Judge determind.

An. 1608. Mr. Richard Harris the next day after he was chosen maior, viz. the 11th of october, required of me (being the town clarke) the seale, with wch I used to seale all proces and precepts concerning his majestyes court in towne; wch I delivered up unto him: he made the most part beleeve that the cause was he would have no poor people arrested in towne; and afterwards of every proces that went forth of the court and was brought to him to be sealed, he doth take 4d. more then

225. The parish register noted 'in the year of our Lord God 1607 in Januarie the ryver of Barnstaple was so frozen that manye hundred people did walke over hande in hand from the bridge unto Castell Rocke with staves in their hands as safe as they could goe on the drye grounde, being the very same mounth the flood was.': NDRO, Barnstaple parish register.

hath been accustomed to be paid. Now let every man judge whether this new order never used before in Barum by Mr Maior, were for remorse he had to the poor or for his own gaine.

—the affair opend by Riley, but interrupted by the Judg as they thought he did not tell his Tale, as they say he should & scarce any Sentence that came from the Judge but was a shock to him & the rest of the company, & little said of Mr. Dellbridge's Side, saying that one Pugsley a poor boteman was examynd concerning that one Davy of Tawton had sworn before the Jurie at Exon that by reason of this new worke could not pass the Bridg by night as well as before, whereas in Truth Davy passd the Bridge by nyght many tymes since & Pugsley in companie as Pugsley there constantlie affirmd before the Judg, whc. the Judg did very much consider & then well thought that Matter was carried ag[ains]t the Town of Malice and Displeasure so thare they award that this Busyness shd go no farther: then Richard Ley informed the Judg that by reason of this new work the Channel there was become so deep that Horses cod not pass over to fetch Sand as they usd.

An. 1609 Notwithstanding the aboundance of corne of all sortes that hath come by water to this towne to the quantitie of 29 thousand bushels by esteem,[226] *yet the price therof holdeth up, viz. wheat at 10s. Rie and Barley at 6s. the bushell: and they that dwell 20 miles hence repair hither for corne.*

This towne of Barum holdeth the Chauntery of St Anne of the king by socage:[227] *it was bought of Edward the sixth and some other lands by that tenure; for wch by composition made with them the towne paid 20s.*

About Christmas this year the schoolhouse was all within new made and the worke finished. It was new and so well repaired at the only cost and charges of Mr John ['Del' crossed through] *Delbridge who had*

226. By estimation.
227. The tenure of land held by certain determinate services other than knight-service.

been once maior of this towne. Thus far out of Mr Wyat townclarke of Barum, his memorials of the said towns &c.

the ['yar' crossed through]*year is wanting in th booke Adde.* ['the' crossed through] *to the foregoing.*

On Monday being the 28th day of January, Mr Skipham a gentleman of the earle of Bath came to towne and delivered unto Mr Maior a letter from the king dated the 24th day of this January, directed unto the maior, Aldermen and burgesses of Barum: the contents of wch letter were; that wheras his majesty had granted unto this towne a new charter with the increase of our libertyes, that the maior &c should elect the earle of Bath for their recorder to be executed by himselfe or his deputy. &c.[228]

The Saturday in the evening being the 2d day of february [1611] *about nine of the clock dyed sir Richard Smith the ordinary preacher of this towne, and was buryed the tuesday following in the chancell ther*[229] *and Mr John Down the parson of Instow preached at his funerall.*[230]

These 2. memorandums were in a loose leafe belonging to the booke, having no date of the year in it.

Note—This Town of Barnstaple holdeth the Chantery of St. Ann of the Crown by Soccage, it was bought of Edwd 6 and some other Lands by that tenure for wch by Composition the town paid £xx.

228. The letter, dated 24 January 8 James I, remains in the borough collection. The King wrote that 'of great use for the good government of the Town that he should be so and an honour to you that a person of his rank should have it … So if you shall neglect to do it, we shall think our favours lately done to you ill bestowed': NDRO, B1/566.

229. Smith was buried on 5 February 1611: NDRO, Barnstaple parish register.

230. Downe was given £1 by order of the Mayor in 1603: Chanter and Wainwright, *Reprint*, II, 99.

APPENDIX I

The Spirit of the North Devon Journals

The North Devon Magazine containing the Cave and Lundy Review
Volume II (1824), 235–9 [copy held in the Periodical Collection at the Westcountry Studies Library, Exeter. The footnotes appear as in the original.]

THE SPIRIT OF THE NORTH DEVON JOURNALS

How I become acquainted with this representative of the by-gone time, must be buried in oblivion; like Junius, 'I am the depository of my own secret' ... I colloquize with some thin and sheeted manuscript that has arisen from the deep grave of my portfolio, or the innermost recesses of my cabinet.—Philip Wyatt, Town Clerk of Barum, *vade in pacem.*

Come all you Barum constables, come lawyers clerk and gowned clerk!
I've got a little song to sing about a gentle Town-clerk;
And if the name of Philip Wyat mingle in my story,
Tis all with due submission to that old quill-barber's glory.

I'll tell you *why at* him I point the finger of the muses—
That's just nine fingers—as adown the stream of time he cruises,
It is that he hath record left, how Barum town arrayed a
Battalion brave of doughty men to fight *the Don's aramada.*

We may be proud of Barum built when first the Cornish Britons ran,
In courage vainly *pit*ted against the royal Athel*stan*;
No fable that, but yet, I deem, we have more cause for priding
Ourselves, that Barum helped the Dons to *leathering* and *hiding*.

That I have seen the ghost of Barum town-clerk it is true, sirs,
And that which he revealed to me I will reveal to you, sirs;
It was not at the midnight hour, that he appeared to me, sirs,
But on the eve of summer's day, as fine as you shall see, sirs.

'Twas sitting in my lodging study deep in pensive mood,
In contemplation of a boat that came by *Anchor-wood*;
That boat went down to *Greeson* at morn with motion steady,
But now the *sternest* of her crew were got a little *heady*.

Now whether 'twas the *widdy-waddy* motion of the boat
That little water had imbibed—my fancy set afloat,
But like her crew's a dizziness came o'er my waking eyes
And I saw dimly what awakened much of my surprise.

Just where the evening shadows fell within a book-recess
Upstarted Philip Wyatt, in his old and clerkly dress;
Black was his coat, around his throat there was a ruff and band,
A goose-quill stuck behind his ear—a Journal in his hand.

Three strides he made into the room in front of my tea-table
And I rose up to set a chair—as well as I was able;
Of this he took no notice, but in a tone commanding,
Said 'take your pen and follow me!' then read his journal standing.

I could have said with *Denmark's Prince* 'no farther would I go'[1]
But I saw a cloud of inky hue upon his parchment brow;
I could have asked the clerkly spirit, 'whither wouldst thou lead me?'
But I saw him pull his pen-knife out, and I thought he meant to bleed me!

Bright was its point and keen its edge—my fears 'twere vain to tell ye,
My hand it shook just like a moulded hand of good *rum jelly*[2]
And so, perforce, I took my pen, and wrote as he dictated
And these the deeds of ancient days his Journal Book related

1. Whither wouldst thou lead me? stay, I'll go no farther. Hamlet.
2. Distilled almost to jelly with the effect of fear. Hamlet.

1586[3]

'The beginning of my journal, by the date, I seem to fix
About the fifteenth-hudredth year, increased by eighty-six;
When, first, there was a muster made before my Lord of Bath,
Of able men prepared to march in glory's fatal path.
Nor scarcity of men alone the evil of the year,
For wheat was at eight shillings, and all other corn as dear;
A Chichester and Basset died, and people would repent all,
So divers men and women rode to fast at Pilton trental.
But soon all fasting over, Dick Greynfield brought a ship in,
Deep laden with materials for merry Christmas keeping;
Twas on the seas he met with her, and closely did he hug her,
Until her Donna-ship gave up her ginger and her sugar.

1587

My Lord and Lady Bath they dined with Barum Corporation,
And she the only lady there, a cause of great vexation;
The Corporation volunteered with all their best to treat her,
But not a lady in the town was ever asked to meet her,
So while from the Guildhall went forth a sound of dishes clattering,
Thro' Barum Streets was hears a clang of angry women chattering;
To this, however, scarce a man of all their husbands listened;
Wheat was cheaper; and the Baby Bath was Bobby christened.

1588

Wheat was cheaper still; but fears of cruel Don's invasion,
And vessels were prepared to serve Sir Francis Drake's occasion;
And when they sailed brave wishes went with them across the bar,
While soldiers on the Castle-green were viewed for coming war.
Great Barum bridge from wood to stone exchanged its northern pier,
At six-and-twenty pounds expense—in those times rather dear;
Another thing occurred of not, at Easter (plainly clerk it!)
More than a hundred oxen fat were brought to Friday's market.

3. See the North Devon Magazine, Vol. II, pages 153–5.

1589

In this year Robert Apsley, senior, gave the Town great charity;
Lord Bath, too, who had dined here, deeming food no rarity,
Gave orders for a lot of wheat, of butter, and of cheese,
To set the great Sir Francis Drake's bold stomach at its ease.

1590

The plague was raging—and assize was held in the Quay-hall,
On Castle Green, too, there was built a gibbet grim and tall;
Sir Robert Anderson, the judge, his jury well harangued,
And eighteen prisoners, at once, for murder were up-hanged.
Yet slight on men was the effect of such severe example,
On mercy, or severity, will villains always trample,
One Edward Chichester, ere long, in some dispute, or swagger,
Was cruelly and foully slain by Captain Gamon's dagger.
This year was most eventful as of any I shall tell,
Eight ships were sent across the bar to fight at far Rochelle;
And one across the bar came in, the Prudence she was named,
And well her owner might avow her title never shamed.
She had the Prudence to pick up a prize on Guinea's coast,
Oh! never such a prize before could Barum's harbour boast!
The list of all she won and wore—I may not stay to give it,
But her hold was full of chests of gold, her sails perfumed with civet!

1591

Once more the worth of Prudence learn, across the bar she bounds,
And soon brings home another prize, worth just 10,000 pounds;
The price of cider hogsheads now at market thrice a shilling,
And watchmen were employed to keep the plague from people killing.

1592–1593

The first of these two years the town with plague was little tainted,
And then they bought a set of chimes, and had the church new-painted!
And in the summer of the last occured so long a drought,
That Rawleigh mills by Hartland folk for grinding much were sought.

1594–1595

And as it happens oft in life, that fast on ill will rush ill,
Wheat rose in these two years from five to shillings nine per bushel:
The price of rabbits too was raised by Braunton Burrows warreners,
And the two Aldermen became the first of Barum Coroners.
Next came the Earl of Bath in state, the men at arms he ranged,
And all their clumsy English bills for piercing pikes he changed;
Loud fired the calivers and muskets, broke were the bows and arrows,
As useless weapons, only fit for shooking rooks and sparrows.
And then before the year was out Jack Norrys brought from London
A bran new charter for the town—read out, when it was undone,
Before the mayor and common-council, ere they went to dinner,
Wheron the market-clerk elect was Mr Thomas Skinner.'

Much more he had to tell, but when thus far he had proceeded,
Phil. Wyatt in his journal paused, nor farther more areded:
The cause was plain—altho' he could not scent the morning airs[4]
A savoury smell of roasting duck came floating up the stairs.

'In my Book,' he said, 'unless your brains are made of batter,
You'll find, most noble copyist, a fund of stirring matter;
I had much more to read to you, but now 'tis getting late,
And pity 'twere, on my account, your Barum friends should wait.

For, by my nostrils, I perceive my visitation here
May interupt expected friends who share your evening cheer;
And it shall ne'er be said *my spirit* threw a damp on cup, or
Abridged the pleasure to be won from singsong after supper:

So 'fare thee well and if for ever, comrade, fare thee well,'
The voice that calls me to my vault is tongued by evening bell;
But deem not that in idleness within the grave I rust,
My fingers keep a journal still, my annals writ in dust.

Stern are the characters I trace, but by the Holy Rood!
A 'blazon that may never be to eyes of flesh and blood;'
Adieu! adieu! adieu! I hear the click-wheel of thy jack!'
Then he flung his journal at my head, and vanished in a crack.

4. But soft, methinks I scent the morning air. Hamlet.

My books they shook upon their shelves, my tea-things on their tray,
As the clerkly ghost of Philip Wyatt passed in air away;
My senses shook, but up I took his journal from the floor,
Then took a turn on the North-walk to get my panic o'er.

So now you have at your command a key unto the mystery
By which I learned, from other days, the pith of Barum history;
Much may it profit Barum sage, and tutor Barum youth,
That around the poet's fiction there should lie such air of truth!

APPENDIX II

The Chronicle of Richard Wood and Mr Frayne, 1533–1678

North Devon Record Office, B12 Z/1

Abstracted from an old Mss but I can't find out whose memd they are since the above—The Mss was written by Rd Wood vicar of Fremington. & other parts by ... Trayne.

1533 Abbeys put down.
[15]75 Jan. 30 John Ferris baptised
88 new arch builded to the Bridge
1604 Nov. plague in Barnestap.
5 Ap. Tho. Lugg when one of the Bridgewardens & not of the Comon Counsel—Monte Lug was then built
6 Jan. a great flood
7 Dec. a great frost
8 Nichs Long Receiver
1608 Jan. the walking place new made
1609 the churchyard new righted

1610 Dec. a new Charter
1612 Dec. a great shipwreck
13 John Are Receiver
Richd Wood born
15 Matthew Tooker Receiver
18 blazing Star
1619 5 bells in Barnestaple new cast Culpepper Clepham, & Foulkes Down, ch.wardens.
20 Robert King Receiver
23 William Wood Reciever
4 Tobias Hooper Rec.
9 Tho. Horwood Rec.
30 John Blackford Rec.
20 Feb: John Lord Fitzwarren born
1 G. Penrose Rec.
much shipwreck
John Downe parson of Instow died
2 William Wood } [marginal note]
3 Tho. Matthews } Rec[eive]rs
4 Edw. Snell }

8 May 1632 Rd Wood admitted into Exeter College Oxon

1635 Wm Paige
6 John Skitit
7 G Penrose July 25th Richd Wood marrd in Gloucester College
8 Wm Baker
9 Hugh Punchard
40 John Horwood
1 Tho. Dennis Nov. 3 the Parliamt began
2 G. Penrose
3 Wm Walter Recr

[crossed through. 1588] 1628 Henry Downe George Baker bridgwardens. Neither of them being of the Counsel at that tyme it being 27 years from the tyme of Mr. Bakers being Maior to the Time that he was Bridgwarden So that if he had been of the Common Council he must have been Maior long before and therefore cannot plead Antiquity that the Bridgwardens were always of the common Counsel.

1644. Memdm. That the 1 day of July 1644 a day never to be forgotton by the Inhabitants of Barnestaple for Gods Mercie & favor shewed in that miraculous delivance of them from that bloody Conspiracy of some of our

Neighbours in inviting & bringing in 5 or 600 horse & foot being French Irish & some English agt the said town with purpose to have put all therein to the Sword and to have possed themselves of the whole Town But were repulsed & driven away by the small power the Townsmen had, our warning & notice was but two Days before—on the 9th July one Howard a Lieutenant who was taken prisoner in the fight was hanged at the Highcross of Barnestaple.

Memdm. that the .... day of October in the Morning Charles Peard being Maior absented himself & wd not appear to yield up his Office whereupon he was dismyssd from his Maioralty & fined by the Town & Henry Masson elected who within three Hours surrenderd his Maioralty again unto Adam Lugg who was sworn Maior then presently for the Year ensuing. 3 Maiors in one day.

1645 Joseph Delbridge Recr.

1646 Apr. the great Plague.

July. I and my Family went to remayn at Rookebear.

Sepr. Mr. Ferris was elected Maior on the Marsh on the higher Side of Konybridge by Ballets.

Dec. I and my family retornd into our own habitation at Barnestaple.

Oct. Hugh Howley Esqr. was bd.

William Wood Receiver

1647 John Cook Recr.

Mr. Richd. Harris was dismissd two years before his Death from being of the Common Counsel & Mr. Paige put in for him.

—Harris took the Vane from the Chapple at Litchdon [Litchardon] Almshouse & placed it on the Keyhall.

1648 Rd Hooper Rec.

Dec. 26 Richard Wood was actually possessd of the Vicarage of Fremington. 1649 John Cooke Recr.

50 John Tucker junr. Rec.

1650. Mr. Hugh Horsham Maior cod. not write his name.

51 Wm Punchard Rec.

1651. Mr. Thos. Dennys Maior—was psecuted by one Daniel Cary & was outed of his Mayoralty for being chosen Captn. of the Traind Bands the Town being then for the King when he was chosen Captn.

1652 John Seldon Rec.

1653 Barth. Bissd Rec.

23 Novr. My cousin John Chechester Rector of Alverdiscott died

1654 Nath Symons Recr.
Jan. John Slowley Esqr died
1655. My Lord of Bathe died[5]
1655. Aug. Coll. Penruddick & Col. Groves beheaded in the Castle of Exeter. 1655. 16 Aug. I appeared before the Commissioners at the New Inn in Exon & was then outed of my vicaridge. set over
my uncle Giles Rect. of Monkohampton died
1656 Nath. Hooper Rec.
1657 [crossed through. Jo. Trayne Rec.] George Rooke

1658 no receiver, the Maior Joce Danil Cary, but the town wd. not admit of him, he being a turbulent and seditious fellow.
1659 25 June I took Possession of my Church of fremyngton.
1661 Jas. Lugg Rec.—then Corporn. new modelld according to Act of P.
There was removd Mr. Nichs. Cooke & Mr. Paige placd. in his room, Mr. John Cooke & Mr. Xpher Hunt in his room—Mr. Thos. Bisseland & Mr. Thos. Coles in his room, Mr Richd Harris & Mr Ackland in his room, Mr. Tho. Cox and Mr. Lewis Rosier in his room. Mr. John Rosier placed in Mr. Cox office of Town Clerk.
1662.—Rawleigh Clapham Rec.
1664.—Richard Salisbury Recr—Seldon no Maior by the Act—not having recd. the Sacramt. in one Year before chosen.
1664.—About the Beginning of March Wheat was sold in the Market for 4:10d. & 4:8d. pr. bl. but in a fortnight after it was sold for 7:6—it was occasiond by reason that one Mr. George Burgoyne & Giles Boyen and others did ingross Corn in the Country & carried it away by water.
1665—7 March Sr. John Chechester of *Rawleigh* was sworren Recorder Mr. Basset being put into that place by the Comr. for regulating Corporations but not approved of by the Corporation, on the 15 May by Mr. Henry Langford brought a Mandamus to shew Cause why he shd. not be admitted Recorder.
—Mr. Bassett overthrone by a trial at Exon.
July Dr Henry Down Dr of Physic died
14 Octr. Mr. John Palmer sworn Maior but no Receiver sworn at time of his swearing.
—there was great discution betwixt the Majestrates

5. Henry, fifth earl of Bath, died 16 August 1654 and was buried the following day.

—Seldon, Ackland Paige & others forsaking the Bench & refused to sit at the Maiors table, which gave the Maior occasion to keep no Court Dinners that year.
1666.—July. they warnd a hall to chuse new Majistrates at wch Time there was great decention began by Mr. Seldon, Ackland & Paige concerning their pretended Seniority—Ackland Lewis Rosier Chr: Hunt T. Colles and Gilbert Paige being put in by the Comr. for regulating Corpns. would take place before those wch had been antient Magistrates nay some of them Maior many years before, but the Corporation wd. not allow of it, the new Company protested against it (a deed of Insolency) & in former days [crossed through. who] wd. have been punishd, either by disfranchisment or binding them over to answer at the Assizes for that there contempt of the Power granted by the Charter, but the Maior pceeded & Tho. Harris was elected a Comon Council-man in room of Mr. John Horwood who died & was buried the 21.
—Mr. John Greade Maior.
—John Fairchild Receiver—Gread was Serjt. at mace many years & now the Serjt. sits in the Maior's place & is not this Topsyturvy.
1667.—Ed. Stanley Recr.
my wife Elenor Trayne died 20 Sept. 1667 & buried at Northam.
1668.—Henry Traine Receiver
9 Tho. Lugg Recr.
1678.—Mr. Richd. Salsbury Maier began the building of Pilton Bridge.

INDEX

LIST OF SUBSCRIBERS

Revd R.J.P. Acworth
Mrs A. Adams
Mrs Adams
Mrs J. Aiken
Mrs R.E. Allen
Mr R.D. Andrew
Mr N. Annett
Mr T. Arkell
Mr A.G. Ashwick
The North Devon Athenaeum
Dr B. Attock
Mr J.L. Attwood
Mr A.J. Babbage
Mrs G. Badcock
Mrs M. Baker
Miss C. Baker
Miss S. Baker
Mr B.J. Bament
Mr M.W. Barker
Dr A. Barlow
Barnstaple Town Council
Mr R.H. Barraclough
Ms E. Barrington
Miss A. Barton
Mr J.C. Baxter
Mr and Mrs R.H. Beattie
Dr R.N. Beck
Mrs C. Bedford
Miss M.L. Beer
Mr N. Beer
Mr N. Beer
Miss C.F. Belam
Mr A.F. Bennett
Mrs A.C.H. Berry
Dr S. Bhanji
Mrs I. Birch
Miss M.E. Bird
Mr A. Bissett
Mr D. Blackman
Mrs B. Blackmore
Mr S. Blaylock
Mr J. Bosanko
Miss L. Bourne
Mr P.W. Bowden
Mr R. Branscombe
Mrs S. Bray
Dr M. Brayshay
Mr R.E.G. Brett
Mr B. Britton
Mr D.G. Britton OBE
Mrs M.T. Britton
Mr B. and Mrs A. Brock
Mrs R. Brockman
Mr R. Brough
Mr C.J. Brown
Mrs S. Brown
Mr J.R. Brumwell
Mrs M. Budd
Mrs S. Budge
Mr J.F. Bulleid
Mr B.L. Burgess
Mr R.T. Burman
Dr S. Burnett
Mr J.C. Burr
Mr K.J. Burrow
Mr S. Burthyk
Mr R. Butler
Dr A. Cameron
Mrs P. Cantle
Dr B.J. Carter
Mrs M. Channon
Miss E.M. Chapman
Mr R.F. Chapple
Mr R. and P. Chapple
Miss S. Child
Mr A. Chittock
Mr P. Christie
Mr and Mrs B.J. Chugg
Mrs M.C. Clarke
Mr P. Claughton
Mrs Y. Cleave
Mrs D.J. Cleaver
Mrs S. Clements
Mr R.G. Cobley
Mr A.G. Collings
Mr P.R. Collins
Mr D. Connett
Mr C. Cornford
Mr M. Courtney
Mr D.J. Cox
Mr J.D. Cox
Mrs N. Cox
Mr W.P. Cox
Mr D.J.B. Coulter
Dr and Mrs H.E. Cramp
Capt. K.R. Crocombe
Mrs G. Crowther
Miss M. Curry
Mrs J. Dadd
Mr B. Darch
Mr B. Davies
Mr R.J. Dawe
Mrs J. Dawson
Mr G. Denley
Mr C. Dennis